I AM
Always
WITH YOU

DIANE BARTON

ISBN 978-1-63630-096-2 (Paperback)
ISBN 978-1-63630-097-9 (Digital)

All Scripture, unless otherwise stated, is taken from the
New International Version (NIV) of the Holy Bible.

Covenant Books, Inc.
11661 Hwy 707
Murrells Inlet, SC 29576
www.covenantbooks.com

To my dad, Ted Koehl, who showed me that God can change our hearts and use us for His purpose. Thank you for being a man of God and a patient, yet zany, father. My mom, Fran Koehl, who showed me how to love others unconditionally and modeled forgiveness. You are a truly heavenly treasure!

PROLOGUE

In the depths of despair, I remember how I felt when I was alone. I was grieving. My second husband was gone. His abuse would stop, but my heart could not bear the loneliness. I sat in my living room and sobbed out to God. The tears were dripping from my chin. I was crying so much that I could barely breathe—my body racking from emotional pain, "God, oh God, I need you to hold me!" I shouted to him. "God, I need a hug! I don't want to ask a woman to hold me because that's not the hug I need. I don't need a wimpy girl-armed hug. I need a hug that's big and strong. My dad is in Virginia, but, God, it's what I need *soooooo* badly! I know you are the God of the universe. You made everything, but, God, I know to ask this of you is too much, but, God, please!"

In my pain and sorrow, God answered my prayer. Beyond my dreams, He answered my prayer bigger than I could think possible. I saw God sitting large before me. His lap was huge. I felt him reach down and pick me up and put his arms around me in a fully encompassing hug. I can explain what it was like because when I was a very small child, I was held like this—fully enveloped. How many years had it been since I was that small? But within the Father's arms, I was that small because He is so big that the universe cannot contain Him.

He held me. He held me like when I was a child. Until the sobbing stopped. Until I was calm. He gave me the peace that surpasses all understanding.

I was going to be okay. Nothing is impossible with God. Nothing. Absolutely nothing. If He wants to show up in your living room and hold you, He can and He did that for me.

CHAPTER 1

Going through the Motions of Church

Sundays were church days. No exception. We were Lutheran by heritage. My great-grandfather brought his family, which included my six-year-old grandfather, William Koehl, from Germany to America. I can't imagine coming across the ocean in a boat looking for a better life.

I learned from my great uncle, who was a Lutheran pastor, that my great-grandfather came to America first without his family and worked for five years to earn enough money for their passage. He hadn't planned to be here that long without them, but each time they tried to come to America to be with him, one of the children became sick. Their passage was delayed another year and another year and another year. Every week, my great-grandfather saved his church offering envelopes. He didn't give to the church because reuniting his family in America was his sole mission, but after his family was safely in Michigan, my great-grandfather put a quarter in each of those weekly offering envelopes and brought them to the church and placed them in the offering plate. I like to believe he did it not out of duty but out of desire...a desire to thank God for blessing him. For my whole life, I have held that memory dear and am so proud of this great-grandpa I never knew but love and respect for the sacrifices he gave for his family.

Generations later, I remember sitting in church on Sunday mornings in Kalamazoo, Michigan, listening to adults singing the old hymns of Martin Luther. I remember being amazed at how loud Marian and Jim, two members of the "choir," could sing. The walls of the church were covered on the inside with fieldstone and large timbers, and I think when they sang, I could almost see them shake from the intensity of their voices. I was amazed by their passionate singing of songs, but the words made no sense to me.

Attending church was something we just did—like going to school. I was sure that I wasn't going to like heaven. We are going to praise God for eternity singing these incomprehensible songs? I had this to look forward to? Would I too have my hair in a bun and wear pointy shoes and panty hose? Would I have pink or red lipstick? Had I been old enough to wear a watch, I would have watched the minutes tick away.

Once the singing was done, there was the sermon. Nothing could be more awful. The pastor's words tumbled out and bubbled over my head and continued to drag on until the full twenty minutes were complete. The only thing that saw me through that third of an hour was laying my head on my mother's lap as she gently caressed the outside of my ear leaving me in a quiet stupor until the recessional song arose from the organ and we were free to leave to go to Sunday school! Hallelujah!

I did enjoy Sunday school, and I did believe God was real and I knew He could save me if something went terribly wrong…and one day, it did.

When I was young, things were really different from the way they are now. When Mom went grocery shopping, there was a little play place in Meijer where she could let us hang out while she shopped. There were no babysitters—we just played. No mother went to jail for leaving their kids there. We had fun!

But not every store had a play place, so Mom would ask us if we wanted to stay in the car while she went inside. She locked the doors. No parent went to jail. On one particular day, Mom took us all to the mattress store. Billy was little, so he didn't have a choice to stay in the car, but Heidi and I did. I would guess we were in early elementary school, and as I recall, she was buying mattresses for the two of us, so for sure, we were potty trained. When Mom asked us if we wanted to go in, we told her, "No, we'll stay in the car."

She said that was fine, but she had a rule: "There will be no jumping into the front seat. You have to stay in the middle or the back." We had a big light-blue station wagon that in the future would be stolen from our home and driven headlong into a pond, but at this point, it hadn't gone through that challenge and didn't yet smell like swamp and slimy frogs. So we agreed to Mom's one rule and off she went into the store.

As soon as we saw her body go through the door, we started hopping over the seats. It was fun porpoising back and forth over the middle seat into the back, but soon we were bored because we couldn't both jump over at once. I don't remember which one of us decided that if we could jump from the middle to both the front and back seats at the same time, it was double the fun—probably me because I was old enough to know better.

Everything was fine until the point when one of our feet hit the emergency flasher. The red ticking light started...*click...click...click*. I knew what that meant. I had seen shows like the *Six Million Dollar Man*; I knew we had set off the bomb's detonator. We were going to die!

We had choices to escape certain death. We could run from the car into the store, but Mom told us to stay put. Why we felt that we needed to obey this rule when death was imminent—even though a little rule like jumping over the front seat had already been broken, I don't know. Perhaps being disobedient once was enough. Especially since we were getting a taste of the naturally occurring consequences that came with our disobedience.

So the only logical choice was to pray. Heidi and I got on our knees, folded our little paws, and started to pray to Jesus to save us.

I think I may have been crying. My prayers were so fervent. And God delivered us from death by sending Mom from the store surely only seconds before the bomb went off!

She turned off the emergency flashers and saved our lives. She scolded us because the gig was up—she knew we'd jumped the seat.

But I didn't care about the scolding; all I knew was that Jesus saved me and sent my mom just in time and I would never forget it!

When we moved to Plainwell, we still travelled thirty minutes to the same church. The trip was brutal because there were five of us—Dad, Mom, me, my sister Heidi, and my brother Billy. Mom stayed home doing her dream job of raising us, and my dad worked as an accountant. We had love, but new cars were possessions that would never grace our driveway. We had two vehicles—a truck with one bench seat designed to hold three people and an old jeep with two bucket seats. The blue station wagon was history because it had by now spent a stint at the bottom of the frog pond. When the temperature heated up during the summer, the stench of pond rot settled in our nostrils, so we had to get rid of it—likely to someone old whose sense of smell wasn't too keen. Now there were not enough seat belts to go around—but no one wore seat belts when I was a kid—at least not our family. We had just come through the era of women smoking when they were pregnant, for heaven's sake! Seat belts were not a law.

Heidi and I each had a spot in the jeep sitting on the fender behind the front seats under the roll bar. Dad prided himself on the fact that people loved to stare at his vehicles. Rust was an accent color, and if it got too bad, it was nothing that couldn't be patched by bolting on the side panel from an old washing machine. Jeeps may have shocks, but not the one my dad drove, so every pot hole and bump sent my head ramming into the bar just an inch or two above my head.

By the time we arrived at church, Heidi and I were in tears (well, she was always in tears about something) and my parents were ready to strangle us all. No, Sundays were not my favorite day of the week.

My mom joined her friends in a Bible study. She must have gone when I was in school because I don't remember her being away from us, but I know my dad started calling her a Bible thumper. I didn't really understand what that meant, but I knew it wasn't an endearing term.

Things changed when I was in middle school; it wasn't just Heidi who cried on Sundays. When we would get to church, Mom and Dad would drop Heidi and me off, and then they would leave. When they came back to pick us up, I could tell from Mom's puffy eyes and red face that she had been crying. I could tell things were not okay, but we didn't talk about "things." The Thumper rule, "If you haven't got something nice to say, don't say nothin' at all!" was always the way it was.

I can't say it was a terrible thing because my parents applied the same rule to every circumstance, so I was never berated or treated negatively. We were loved. Not spoiled, but loved.

We had respect for our parents. When I was little, I remember when I did something wrong, Dad would take off his belt, fold it in half, and holding the ends of the belt in his left hand, he would put his thumb through the loop on his right hand and he would snap the leather together. It scared the bejeebies out of me! Did he whip me with it? Not that I ever remembered, but he could have! There was respect—respect for what Dad could do to me. We did get spanked when we were small—a couple of swats on the butt. It didn't kill me; it made me listen and do what I was told. Did I hate my parents for it? No, I deserved it and I likely didn't do "that" again!

When I got too old for spankings, we'd talk. When I misbehaved (only once or twice—pffft!), Dad told me to go to my room "to think about it"—which I did. I'd go to my bedroom and lay on my bed, stare up at the ceiling, and think about what I'd done. About an hour later, Dad would come to my room and sit on the edge of the bed and we'd "talk about it." He'd make sure I was put back together and I was okay; there would be a conversation. They never grounded me; they didn't need to. I always knew after the conversation we were all right. I think grounding is so much less effective because it just causes resentment for both parents and kids.

God says not to let the sun go down on our anger—that should apply to parents and kids both. Forgiveness is not just for adults. God says to forgive each other; when God says it, we should do it because He is wise and loving. Forgiveness means it's done. We start new. My parents gave me the gift of always starting new. After an hour, Dad would come sit on my bed and we would talk it through and I'd be all better. I was blessed that way. Dad later told me he had regrets because he didn't teach us to argue or stand up for ourselves, but I was and am unconditionally loved by my parents. I think they got it right.

The only thing I would have changed was within myself. I had guilt from thinking about it, and I had forgiveness from my parents, but I didn't forgive myself. The guilt and lack of self-forgiveness would carry on and affect me for a long time. My parents didn't put this guilt on me nor did it come from church. I believe that Satan put this guilt on me to make me feel like I was not worthy to be a child of God, and this was and is not true. Satan is a liar and he will do everything he can to make us doubt and feel less than we are—a creation of God Almighty. John 3:16–21 states,

> For God so loved the world [you and me] that He gave his one and only Son, that whoever believes in him shall not perish but have eternal life. For God did not send his Son into the world to condemn the world, but to save the world through him. Whoever believes I him is not condemned, but whoever does not believe stands condemned already because he has not believed in the name of God's one and only Son. This is the verdict: Light has come into the world, but men loved darkness instead of light because their deeds were evil. Everyone who does evil hates the light, and will not come into the light for fear that his deeds will be exposed. But whoever lives by the truth comes into the light so that it may be seen plainly what he has done has been done through God.

Please, when you are reading this, hear this loud and clear. God's grace means He forgives us even though we don't deserve it because He loves us. It's done. He died on the cross and took it all away—we are justified through faith. Justified means it's like it never happened (*just* as *if* I'd never done it). When we repent, He erases it all. He washes us clean. God said it in 1 John 1:9: "If we confess our sins, he is faithful and just and will forgive us our sins and purify us from all unrighteousness." We need to believe it for ourselves. It's gone. It's okay to move on unburdened with guilt. He makes us whole. We are clean. We are beautiful and God loves us. Make sure to note the word *all*. We are purified from *all*, not just the slightly not so bad things like jumping over the front seat of the station wagon—*all* of our sins.

Yes, it's important to be sorry; it's important to learn from what we did. But then, we move on—forgiven, unburdened, whole. We are God's beautiful creation—each and every single one of us. He doesn't like it when we judge—even ourselves. Like they say in *Frozen*, "Let it go! Let it go!" We are set free; be free indeed.

Home was safe, except when I got to middle school… Then on Sundays, Momma would cry.

CHAPTER 2

God Gave My Daddy Back

Rides home from church were quiet; sometimes Dad would take a detour and we'd drive through Lake Doster to look at the rich and fancy new houses. When I see those houses now, it makes me laugh— they were two-story homes—it's just we were born in the years of the single-story ranch!

Sometimes Dad would drive in the country, put the Jeep in four-wheel drive, and scale dirt hills. I hated it! Scared me out of my mind, but I'm sure Dad thought it was fun. Driving home, we were in no hurry—there wasn't the stress of getting to church on time. When we got home, everything was sort of back to normal, and we forgot about the tender spots on our head that resulted from the skull to steel impact. We had a simple Sunday dinner and would sit around talking about what had happened during the week.

But something wasn't quite right.

I was about twelve years old, and I realized that Dad would not come home right after work. I would sometimes be in bed, and it would be dark when he would drive up and I could finally sleep knowing he was home. I was old enough to know that my parents weren't happy. I had a feeling my dad had a girlfriend, but I didn't really know. Things were just unspoken. Mom was good about never speaking badly about my dad, but I could feel something wasn't right. I was concerned. Mom later shared with me that she knew God was with her during these hard times. I later learned that my dad had repeatedly asked her for a divorce and she told him no.

Mom's Bible study friends were lifting her up in prayer giving her strength. She told me that one day when she was especially sad, she was sitting on the potty, the only place she had a chance to escape from us kids. As she sat there alone in her tears calling out to God, she said the most amazing song came out of her mouth. It was in a language and voice that was not her own. I know that in the depths of despair, God is always with us and I know my mom has never been able to sing well, but all things are possible with God even something so miraculous as this—singing in tongues! He gave her strength to endure the rejection.

Some people I know believe in speaking in tongues and some think it's utter folly, but I do not doubt that my mother had this experience. God knew this would speak to my mom at her point of deep sadness, so He let her know He was there.

When people say "That was a coincidence," I assure you that when God is doing something and we're open, He will let us know absolutely positively, these are not coincidences, and they are God moments. He tells us, "I am still real. I am here. I am with you." He was with my mom.

But even though God was present in my mom's life, and after years of praying, she lacked the strength to continue in a loveless marriage. My mom finally told my dad he could go. That same day, my dad's boss told him that if he did not shape up, he would lose his job. Then, the final blow, his mistress told him she was leaving him because he wouldn't divorce my mom. Everything important was being ripped from him.

My Bible-thumping mom had given Dad a Bible years before—a Bible he never read. He took that Bible and put it on the shelf above his desk at work to be disregarded and forgotten…until the moment he needed to know if the God of Sundays was real. Broken, sitting in his office, he took that Bible down off the shelf and said, "God, if you're real, I need you now." He took a ruler and slammed it into the Bible and opened it to Colossians 3. God spoke to Dad through this whole chapter. Yes, in all of Dad's ugliness and sin, God promised forgiveness and rescue.

I remember that day because after my dad drove up the driveway, he came to my room and sat on the edge of my bed and he said, "I know you are old enough to know what has been going on and I want you to know that everything is going to be okay," and he hugged me. God brought my daddy back to me.

Things definitely changed because my dad was a man forgiven by God. He had always said prayers before dinner, but now he said prayers with a passion. Tears fell from his eyes, down his face and dripped from his chin into his mashed potatoes…every single meal!—well, not always into his mashed potatoes. Sometimes we had corn. He was not the same man.

Mom bought some nice dresses, and they started to go on dates.

I learned later from Mom that she had gone to Dad's girlfriend and told her she forgave her. She certainly forgave Dad. She is a big lady in a very short body.

Would it have been easier for mom to not forgive dad? Not at all. She loved my dad. Absolutely he hurt her. He betrayed her, but the desire of her heart was to have their marriage restored. God was able. Besides she had something to gain bigger than my dad—forgiveness for herself too. "For if you forgive other people when they sin against you, your heavenly Father will also forgive you. But if you do not forgive others their sins, your Father will not forgive your sins" (Matt. 6:14–15 NIV).

Is forgiving easy? Not at all, but God lifts the burden. Besides, carrying that hurt and resentment around is work. It's a heavy load! It can consume and flatten us, but if we ask God to give us the strength to forgive, He will and it's the biggest weight loss I've ever known. Leave the pain behind for Jesus to deal with; judging is His job, not ours. Move along unburdened.

With the good came the dread—church was no longer just for Sundays. We attended every Christian concert and speaking event. Dad couldn't get enough. It was okay though because the music was different than the songs I heard in my Lutheran church—I could sing them and I started to comprehend the messages…

CHAPTER 3

Jesus Claims Me

The year was 1976, and I was thirteen years old. We were going as a family to hear Dr. Jack Van Impe at Wings Stadium. I remember our chairs were down on the ice which had been covered with a tarp. It wasn't cold and I wasn't distracted away from the message being preached—for the first time in my life, I comprehended and listened to the words being taught from the pulpit. This was very different from church on Sunday.

Lutherans don't have alter calls, but when Dr. Van Impe asked if anyone wanted to give their heart to Jesus, I felt the Holy Spirit grab hold of my heart and pull. I was not going to ignore it. I stood on my feet and tried to go past my family up to the front of that huge auditorium. As I got in front of Dad, he looked at me, and in all innocence, he asked me, "Where are you going?" I looked him in the eyes and said, "I'm going up there!" Shock covered his face—"Oh!" and he quickly moved his legs so I could pass. I mean, seriously, wasn't that the point? In his defense, during the sermon at church, I miraculously had to pee halfway through—my escape from the boredom. I'm sure Dad thought this was just another pee moment. But I would have wet myself in my chair rather than miss one word from Jack's mouth—from God's mouth—to my ears.

Even though that was over forty years ago, I still remember the experience. They took us to a quiet room and asked us if we wanted to pray. I nodded my head yes, but the words could not come from

17

my mouth. I was overflowing with emotion and I could only cry—hard. The nice man prayed the words for me as I sobbed feeling completely full in a way that I had never felt before. He gave me two tracts, which I still have to this day.

I emerged from that room and my parents were waiting there for me. I remember Dad smiling and asking me, "What did you do?" and I just cried some more. I now understood Dad crying in the mashed potatoes. Being filled with the Holy Spirit in my heart, I was really overfilled and overflowing and it's never stopped! To this day, I still have a tearful problem when it comes to things of the Lord!

Just like Dad, I couldn't get enough of being fed. Mom and Dad bought me my own Good News Bible and I read it every night. I couldn't go to sleep until I read three chapters. I started going with my Baptist best friend to youth group and Sunday night church where I couldn't get enough fire and brimstone. All that was good unless you were my Lutheran pastor.

I was in eighth grade, the final year of confirmation in the church. Unfortunately for Pastor Al, I was on fire and there was no dousing it. I remember badgering him passionately in front of our whole class about the importance of having a personal relationship with God. He agreed it was a good thing, but it was not necessary and all people will not have this. I argued terribly with him. I chuckle to myself now wondering what he thought of such spunk from a previously quiet and bored student. Blame Dr. Van Impe, Pastor Al!

I was definitely the most saved kid. Every Sunday evening as I went with my best friend, Anne, to her Baptist church, at the end of the message, her pastor or the youth leader would tell us to bow our heads and close our eyes. He would ask us if we wanted to ask Jesus into our hearts. I'd close my eyes, never peeking because only sinners peek, and I'd raise my hand. If he asked four times in one service, I raised my hand four times! He'd say, "I see you, young lady!" and I'd still raise my hand again because I didn't know he was talking to me because I wasn't peeking. My, I thought he was saving so many every week and now I chuckle to think how he was probably shaking his head in wonder—if they kept count of every person they'd saved, did they count me seven times seventy times? Yep, as my dad said, I had become a "Lutherist"!

It is so incredible to me to think about what happens to us when the Holy Spirit comes alive within us. I think about Saul in the New Testament and how he would do everything within his control to persecute the believers. He hated them, destroying them and all they represented, was his passion. He knew of the miracles of Christ. He couldn't deny it, but he wanted to stop it and was willing to imprison and kill to do it. And then, one day, on the road to Damascus, God spoke to him and it was over. In an instant.

Nothing made sense to him until God arrived and then, wow—complete change.

If you have been shutting Him out, closing the door or your eyes to Him, my prayer for you is that one day, if it's now or tomorrow or next year, when He knocks, open the door. Oh what a Guest you will have in your heart.

When people ask, does He really live in your heart? I can say, in mine that is so. I feel Him like He is increasing my chest capacity. There is no emptiness—it's a fullness. That's the only way to explain it. And, when His presence is too much, the part of Him I can't fit in there anymore, comes out through my tear ducts.

If this type of tearful thing makes you nervous, don't sit by me during a baptism or a good sermon when the Holy Spirit is really moving because I'll be crying. There's just not room in my five-foot, three-and-three-fourth-inch self to hold Him in!

Do you want Him to fill you? I believe He is always there. I picture Him standing behind me. He is close enough for me to touch Him if I reach my hand out, but I need to reach—we have a choice. He doesn't mug us into faith in Him. Afraid to reach, just call Him…"Jesus?"

"I'm here. Come to Me." Do you hear Him? Go and let Him in…

Dear Jesus, I need You. I am a sinner and on my own I can do nothing. I believe in You as my Savior and I ask You, I beg You, to come into my heart and be my Lord. Please forgive me my sins and wash me new each and every day. I will fail, but I give myself to You knowing You will wash me clean. There is nothing I can do to make You leave me. I am Yours forever until you come in Your glory to take me home to be with You forever. I love You, Lord! Amen.

CHAPTER 4

Growing Up on the Farm

Mom came from town and Dad was from the country. Town was really a small village, Colon, the lower bowel of Michigan and the magic capital of the world. Really! Google it.

Both of my parents were in 4-H. Mom planted a garden once. She didn't do too well with it, and when the 4-H kids came to tour it, Mom hid under her bed because the garden was just a bunch of dried-up weeds. Poor Mom!

Dad thought it was very important for us kids to experience 4-H. Since the only club in Plainwell, Michigan, was a horse club and Dad thought there was more to 4-H than horses (sorry, horse people, I know you just fainted!), Dad started our own club.

Dad learned one step ahead of us kids and taught us how to do leathercraft. (Heidi was really good at it and I struggled—surprise). Mom taught cake decorating and clowning. Mrs. Cosgrove, my friend Anne's mom, taught us how to sew. We also learned to bake. All is good except Dad said, if we were in 4-H, we should have animals—especially since we had ten acres. I think all of this was part of Dad's ploy to have animals because remember, Mom was from town and I think she only ever had a dog. So Dad had to do some manipulating: "It's for the kids!" No, it was really for Dad, but Mom must never find out.

Pawnee

I did have a horse. Grandma Van bought her for us. The horse was on her way to the Shipshewana Horse Auction to be sold for glue when Grandma saved her life. Her name was Pawnee and she was an albino. She had blue eyes and no pigment in her skin or hooves. Honestly, she was kind of ugly because her skin was pink and her hair was white, but she was our horse and I loved her. The saddle Dad bought for her cost more than the horse—I think Grandma only paid $100 for her.

Dad had horses growing up, so it was only natural that we should have one except Pawnee bucked everyone off. I managed to stay on except one time when she puffed up when I was cinching up her saddle and I didn't know it. After I got onto her back, she bolted across the fields exhaling with every step. Her saddle slipped sideways, and I slid along with it. When I was parallel to the ground, I jumped, hitting my head on a rock. Dad caught up with us and thankfully I was okay. He realized that part of her bridle had come unhooked, so she didn't respond when I tried to stop her.

The people that sold Grandma Pawnee called us some years after we got her and asked to buy her back at a profit. We learned that she was a Lipizzan and we also learned she had never been broke. That explained why she was initially so inexpensive and also why she misbehaved for most everyone—no one had ever trained her—except me, I guess.

Since we only had Pawnee and no other horse, I had to ride alone which wasn't fun and probably wasn't really safe. There was a stallion next door at Mr. Turcott's and that stud (the horse, not Mr. Turcott) would follow us snorting as we walked past his pasture on the way to the road. He scared me. After a few years, Pawnee just became a pet that grazed and helped facilitate my bicep development as I cleaned her stall in my bare feet (until dad yelled at me that I could puncture my foot and it would get infected if I shoved poop through a wound). I was stubborn, but that was logical, so I wore boots after that.

When I got older, I agreed that Dad could sell her. I don't know where she went, but every time I saw an albino horse at a fair, I'd cry and think it may be her.

Chickens

Dad built the barn soon after they purchased property from Mr. Turcott so we'd have a place to store all our stuff as he finished the house. There was a hammock in the middle of the mess, and a dear sweet hen had decided to lay her nest under it. Mom noticed her, and every day that she went to the barn, she'd lift up the edge of the hammock and talk sweetly to her.

Two weeks of checking on the hen and Mom noticed something terrible—she wasn't sitting on a nest; her leg was stuck in one of the hammock strings and she couldn't move! Every day, the sweet girl thought Mom was coming to save her only to have her hopes of survival dashed again.

Mom ran and grabbed a bowl of water and held it out to her. She gulped and gulped the water as fast as she could. Mom then got her unstuck from the strings and she was free at last.

I don't know how she ever survived that long, but she did. Salvation in the truest sense!

We had lots of little hens, and they laid the prettiest small brown and light-blue eggs. I once told my city friend that all chicken eggs were blue or brown. I explained that some chickens bled from the outside when they laid their eggs—the blood they bled was oxygenated, so the red blood stained the egg brown. Other hens bled from the inside when they laid their eggs—the blood they bled was deoxygenated, so the blue blood stained the egg blue. I finished off my story by telling her that the eggs in the store were all bleached so she wouldn't see the blood. She said, "Oh, I never knew that!" Ha—she so believed me!

We also had guinea hens that made a terrible raucous and loved to perch in the window outside of my bedroom. I really didn't like those birds even though they were very cool looking.

At some point, Mom and Dad realized that there were fewer eggs laid each day than hens and Dad figured that the old hens were no longer laying. It was time to butcher a few and have them for meat. Nooo! I couldn't bear the thought of them dying! This is the girl that would stand in front of a rat hole when Dad filled their holes with water forcing them to exit at the other end of the tunnel so he could shoot them when they ran out. I'd stand in front of the exit and tell him he'd have to shoot me first if he wanted to get to the rats. Yes, I was a little extreme! The rats ate Dad's corn stash meant for the animals. But I'd read *Charlotte's Web*! It could be Templeton!

On butchering day, I went to my room and put my head under my pillow and cried. Sadly, most of the old hens he butchered were filled with eggs. Apparently, the younger ones were the slackers. I knew he shouldn't do it! I knew it! Sniff!

Henry J Peeper Bird

Mom and Dad were in a small group Bible study in town, and one of the families had a daughter whose boyfriend bought her a duck for Easter. Sweet, except she had no place to raise it. Much to our delight, Dad agreed to take the duckling.

Note, we didn't have a pond or anything, so Dad threw him in the toilet. I was horrified, but the duck loved it. He rescued it after I was done having a fit. Dad filled the canoe in the backyard with water and that was his makeshift lake.

I called him Henry J Peeper Bird. Why? Because that was his name, of course!

He was really tame, and he would follow us everywhere. He was big, and he loved to sit on my lap. Because Dad thought he would be happier with other ducks, Dad talked to a lady he knew and asked if she would take him. Dad told me that she had a big pond and he'd have friends, but I wouldn't budge. Probably if I'd have seen her home, I would have been okay with it, but the only place I had ever been that had ducks was Milham Park in Kalamazoo. I told Dad I'd be okay if we took him there.

We got in the car and Henry J Pepper Bird sat on my lap, and we drove him to the park. We let him out next to the other ducks, and I guess I thought he'd say, "Oh, my family, I am here!" and run off to them, but he didn't. I was his family. When we left him to go to the car, he took off across the creek and was waiting for us when we reached the car. So we took him back to the other ducks once again. We left him, and he came waddling at full speed behind us. We literally had to run, slam the doors, and drive off. Horrible! Absolutely horrible!

Why didn't we pick him back up and take him to Dad's friend's house? I don't know? It still hurts my heart. But there is more…

Years later, when I was working, I was sharing my dumb animal stories with some girlfriends (the same ones that believed my colored egg story), and I talked about Henry J Peeper Bird. One of my friends got wide-eyed and asked me, "When was this?" We figured out as best we could about what year it would have been. She said, "Diane, oh my gosh, I think my brother brought him home!" She said it was about that time that her brother went to Milham Park. When he was there, this big white duck kept following him around. When he left to go home, the duck jumped in his car. He took it home and told his mom, "He just got in my car!" His mom didn't believe him (and really why would she, because ducks just don't jump into your car every time you go to the park!). She told him to take the duck back to the park where he found it. It had to have been him!

I wonder how many other people he went home with—yes, creepy people tell me that he probably went home with someone who made him their dinner. I tell myself there will be one duck in heaven and it will be Henry J Peeper Bird!

Sheep

Somewhere along the 4-H journey, my parents met sheep people and Dad successfully convinced my mom that Heidi and I should each raise a lamb. Billy was still too little to have one of his own. Of course, they are so cute, so this was absolutely okay with us.

In the spring, we went to a sheep farmer and picked out our lambs. To exercise them, we walked them down the driveway on leashes like dogs. Although there wasn't much traffic on our country road, we were quite the distraction.

They were so tame. By the time we got to the fair in the fall, we walked around the arena and they just followed us around the show ring. The judge had the nerve to mark us down because we didn't have control of our animals. We asked, "What do you mean? They aren't going anywhere." He said, "Well, they could!" Whatever! They wouldn't leave us any more than Henry J Pepper Bird would!

After a couple of years of buying lambs, Dad told Mom that we couldn't make any money on our lamb project because we paid too much for the lambs in the first place. Part of the lesson was supposed to be how to make money raising livestock. He convinced Mom we needed some ewes. We bought two sweet ladies that we named after Mom's great aunts, Margaret and Evelyn, because they looked similar. Ha! No, we never told Margaret and Evelyn—I don't think they'd be thrilled to know they looked like sheep or sheep looked like them!

Sheep are not easy to raise because they're stupid. When it was time for lambing, Dad would check on the ewes often, and there were times that he had to push them back in before the mom or baby died of distress. When they have babies, they are supposed to dive out of their moms, but it doesn't always work that way. Sometimes they get twisted up inside; a front and back leg could come out together or their heads aren't aimed at the exit and she can't push them out sideways. The cool thing is, God gives lambs white spots on the bottom of their front hooves, so if you have one hoof with white and another without, it's sideways. Push it in and begin again! It sounds so easy unless you're the ewe or Dad who was pushing the lamb back in as she was trying to push it out. Then there's the complication of having legs from two different lambs, twins!

Watching them be born was so stressful. I pushed for her and was exhausted when she was all done. We never lost a baby, but I know it was because Dad and I were really good shepherds. One night at two in the morning, Dad came into the house and said I needed to come out to the barn. One of the lambs was stuck inside its mom's birth canal with its head tipped backward. Dad's arms were too big and he couldn't get up in there to turn the head. Someone had to push their arm up there and turn its head around—I was going to have to do it. I reached up inside of her and felt the head and turned it toward me. Once I did that, she slipped right out. After she was done delivering both the babies and the afterbirth and she stopped contracting, we would put antibiotics up inside of her uterus so she didn't get infection. Dad told me, "You need to do it because she is closing back up again and your arm is much smaller than mine. I'm afraid I'll hurt her." I did it right away—I couldn't bear to have Dad hurt her; she'd been through so much already. I can say I've been armpit deep inside a sheep!

We went to a lot of meetings with other lamb 4-H people learning about the process. The Southerland family was extremely helpful. I loved going to their house to hear the stories. One in particular was interesting in a disgusting sort of way!

Bernie Southerland was quite a character. He told us of a veterinarian whose very attractive wife castrated lambs with her teeth. The process of castration that we were supposed to use was to cut off the end of their scrotum, save the little piece of fur and skin, and dry it to later use as a Barbie doll hat. Then we reach up, grab the testicle, and rip it from the lamb's body. Apparently, the lambs don't enjoy the process, so they'd pull their testicle back up inside when someone tried to pull it out. Since the testicle is slippery, supposedly, the vet's wife found it easier to clamp on to the testicle with her teeth instead of using her fingers. As a kid, the whole conversation was uncomfortable and I was quite sure that Bernie was just telling a story because he could.

Well, there finally came a day when we had our first male lamb. Dad had paid attention to Bernie and the details of castration (minus the teeth). Mom held the lamb—holding a front and back leg in each hand with the lamb's butt facing up so Dad could do his thing. Dad sliced off the end of the scrotum (I don't know that he saved the piece for a Barbie doll hat or not, but I seemed to think they did—a conversation "piece" if nothing else). He tried to grab the testicle, but he couldn't—the lamb was sucking them back inside.

Mom and Dad switched places because Mom had to try—I guess we women always think we can do things better? After not a lot of luck, Dad jokingly yelled to Mom, "Use your teeth!" She did! Absolutely completely disgusting, but it worked. She backed off from the sheep with a testicle and blood hanging from her teeth.

I'm not sure who fainted first—my dad or the sheep, but Mom came inside and asked for a kiss. Barf!

After that day, Mom and Dad always prayed for females.

Whenever Heidi had a boy over, either Dad didn't particularly like him or he wanted to make sure he could tolerate our sense of humor. Dad would set down his napkin after he finished his meal, look the boy in the eye, and ask, "Did you know Fran castrates lambs with her teeth?" The young man would nervously laugh and say, "Right!" Mom would reply, "Yep, I do," and would snap her teeth together. Haaaa! I loved growing up on a farm. Some guys didn't come back. Only the strong survived to date Heidi a second time!

Well, ewes don't just have babies on their own, one must have a ram. We took the ladies on vacation to visit the boy toy the first few years. Then Bernie told Dad that he would sell him his ram. Dad told Mom we were just borrowing him, but that wasn't exactly the whole story; he just didn't tell Mom he was ours. His name was Hustler; he had this name because he hustled the ladies. In his line of business, this was a good thing. So soon, our flock was growing.

Hustler couldn't be trusted. We could never turn our back to him because he'd charge and he was pretty big; he could hurt someone. But he had his purpose and he did it well.

Our house was a walkout ranch, and my bedroom was on the corner where the side window was even with the ground. I didn't like to awaken at daybreak, so I tried to convince Mom and Dad to allow me to have a black room. They agreed to let me have black paneling on three walls, but one wall was white wallpaper with black footprints. Grandma Koehl bought me hippy beads to hang in the windows and I had white shades behind the beads. Heidi had pink paint and a white canopy bed because she wasn't as cool as me.

Grandma Van was always worried that boys could get into my room because the window was ground level, but for the record, that never happened—no human boy anyway.

One day when we were all at school and work, Hustler escaped from the barn. He ran up to my window. The shade was pulled down (of course, because I was allergic to waking up!), so when Hustler looked in the window, he saw his reflection. Never having seen his reflection before, he assumed the worst—there was a competitor on his farm! There was only room for one ram, so he did the only thing he could—he set out to rid the farm of the other guy! He put his head down and charged! He destroyed the other ram and my window in the process.

Not to worry, my twin bed was beneath the window, so Hustler had a soft landing and trotted off to spend the rest of the day in our downstairs drinking from the toilet and pooping as animals do.

Billy got home first from school that day, and when he came in the back door, he heard someone in the house. He immediately fled to the barn.

Dad was a dumpster diver at work, and as they replaced phones, he rescued them and brought them home and installed those rotary phones in every room—including the barn and bathrooms. Thankfully, the day that the burglar was in the house, Billy could call Dad from the safety of the barn.

Dad told Billy not to go back into the house but to run to the neighbors and he would drive home from work as fast as he could.

Billy disobeyed and climbed up into the haymow and waited for Dad to arrive. When he did, he told Dad he had been watching the house and no one left.

Dad went to the back door and opened it, and at the first smell, he knew that we didn't have a human burglar. Dad grabbed Hustler and took him out the sliding door in the basement. He was thankful Hustler was a sheep and not a goat because he didn't climb the stairs. Dad yelled to Billy to help him rip up the remnant carpet from the floors as fast as possible before Mom came home and Hustler became stew. "But, Mom, he was just doing his job protecting the ladies!" After Hustler had an experience as a house ram, Mom said he had to go. Thankfully, Dad's Uncle Don, another crazy, sheepish relative, found a local two-legged lady that wanted a ram for her farm, and Hustler moved on to greener pasture.

One year, after I had left home, Mom and Dad had a lamb that was rejected by its mom. She wouldn't feed it, so they did. Mom and Dad were going away overnight and they asked me if I'd come bottle feed the lamb. Of course I would. I got to the barn and found the ewe in the back pen. I shoved her up against the wall and milked her until I filled the Pepsi bottle that was the little one's fake mama. Then I put the nipple on top and let the little lamb eat. "My mama the

Pepsi bottle!" we'd say. I did this a few times over the weekend. That ewe was none too happy about the process, but if she'd have just fed it like a good mama, this wouldn't need to happen!

Mom and Dad got home after their trip and called me in alarm asking, "Didn't you feed the lamb?"

I said, "Yes—three times."

They asked me, "What did you feed her? The formula is still on the freezer in the laundry room where we left it."

"Formula? You had formula? I milked the ewe!" I replied.

Mom and Dad were roaring—"You milked the ewe? How did she take it?"

"Not well!"

I guess, never assume…and ask for the details was the moral of the story!

So what does this have to do with God? I truly know God is with us every day and he loves it when we're happy. Genesis 1 and 2 is wonderful! I think God was most amazing when he made the animals for us to enjoy! "In the garden, he made all of the creatures to be companions for us. But, he found there was no suitable companion, so he made Eve from his rib" *so she could talk to him incessantly and tell him what to do his whole life. When Adam needed a break from Eve's constant babble, he went and sat with the animals. Note: This part in italics isn't in the Bible!—I think God left it out or women would get really mad. Ha!*

CHAPTER 5

Meet Husband Number One

Mom told me I went from being a little girl to a woman and skipped the years in between. She said she wasn't sure why I dated my first husband so long before I married him. Um…because I was still in high school? Oh yeah.

I really was obnoxious toward my family. I was disgusted with my sister, Elizabeth Sue Koehl, who was called Heidi because my dad liked that name (then why wasn't it her name?). One year in elementary, my mom went to parent-teacher conferences and Heidi's teacher kept talking about Elizabeth. My mom stopped her and said, "I'm Heidi's mom." The teacher asked her, "Who is Heidi?" That one year, she used her legal name with her teacher and it was really weird. It must be she decided she was a Heidi because it only lasted for nine months and the next year, she changed from Elizabeth to Heidi again.

Heidi didn't enjoy reading, so that in itself should tell you something was off about her. She was artistic; I couldn't match my clothes. She was thin and I had curves. Heidi was the really pretty one and all of the boys liked her. I used to tease her that she could make a paper chain with the name of each of her admirer's name on each link and it would stretch back and forth across her room. My chain would only be one link.

Billy, my younger brother by six years, was born when my mom lost weight. She didn't stay thin for long; I think Dad noticed her, and next thing I knew, she was having my brother.

Billy was okay and that's being generous. When he was nine, he was actually quite gross. He stunk. He never wanted to wash his butt, and he mixed his clean clothes in with his dirty ones in his clothes hamper. When I would scowl at him and ask him how he knew which ones were which, he'd say, the dirty ones stick to the wall. Ewww. I remember asking my mom if we could give him to foster care. I didn't know why he needed to breathe my air. She told me no, so we kept him and I just left Billy and Heidi to play together. I couldn't relate to them.

It was really okay that they liked each other, and I didn't want to share my air. It gave me time to just stay in my room and read.

My mom is the sweetest lady ever. She is loving and bubbly. She rarely says an unkind word about anyone, but I couldn't see that in my youth—probably typical with most kids. It amazes me how much I was truly insensitive to her feelings. She'd put up with a lot from Dad's unfaithfulness and lack of faith, and I most certainly didn't make it easy on her either.

I remember one time that she said something to make me mad (which as a young teen could have been something like "pass the salt") and I huffed off to my room—you know, the one with the ground-level window that Grandma Van thought boys could enter. I cranked opened the window, took out the screen and set it on the floor, and then went and sat in my closet and closed the door from the inside. After the appropriate cool-off time that my parents always respected, Mom came to check on me. She found the window open and assumed just what I'd hoped—I'd run away. I freaked her out. She sat on my bed and cried.

As a Christian human being, one would think I'd have felt bad, but I sat in the closet and let her cry—what a creep! After a time, she left. After more time, I got out of the closet, put the screen back together, and closed my window. I don't really recall my "homecoming." I am sure there was no killing of a fattened calf, but after forty-plus years, I still remember that I made her cry and it makes me so sad. Teens are creeps at times, and I most definitely earned that title!

When I was in second grade, Mom and Dad started sending Heidi and I to piano lessons. I really liked it. Heidi cried when she had to practice. She cried a lot; Dad called her Pitiful Pearl. She cried so much about piano lessons that Mom and Dad finally gave up and let her quit. It was probably a good choice; they could later use the money for painting lessons and I wasn't good at that. No amount of crying on my part was going to make me understand what colors complement each other. Mom and Dad must have known that because they never paid for one art class for me.

Mom and Dad rented a piano for our lessons at first, but at some point, they realized it was more expensive to rent a piano compared to buying one, so they found this piano tuner guy who fixed up pianos and sold them. We went to his house and I'll never forget what I saw there—he had nice normal wooden pianos, a piano painted antiqued green (an artist must have done it), and this glorious red piano.

You know which piano I wanted! She was from Shakey's Pizza Parlor in Lansing. She was an old upright and the back had been removed so I could see the hammers which were each painted a different color and had thumb tacks pushed in the back so each time I struck the key, the hammer would fire and the tack would hit the string and make the most beautiful honky-tonk sound. The best was yet to come—they had mounted a black light under the lid, and when the lights were off, the hammers with their fluorescent paint just sailed going back and forth! My parents were sure we should get a traditional piano, but here's the dig—she was only $125! Sold!

Imagine my piano instructor Mrs. Pease's delight when she found out I was playing Bach and Beethoven on a red instrument like this. I'm sure it was utter blasphemy in "piano teacher land," but I didn't care.

I truly believe this was the best $125 my parents could have spent because my piano became my teen therapy. When my family drove me to the brink, I disappeared to the basement and started banging out the loudest classical music I could find until my soul soothed and so did the songs. My piano made all things better unlike anything else…until boys.

In addition to piano, I played alto saxophone. I don't think there is a more beautiful looking instrument than the sax—the pearly button keys and the gold contrast—wow. I played in the concert band. In eighth grade, a couple of the guys from the high school came to the middle school and introduced us to jazz band. I loved the change in music and the guy who played sax was not bad looking either.

I wore a bra and started my period when I was ten, but I didn't kiss a boy until seventh grade. I was quite innocent and didn't feel left out at all. I liked boys a lot, but holding hands was just fine—after all, the books I read all just ended with a kiss at the end.

But real kissing—that was taught to me by Stony Smithers in the back of the bus on the way back from music festival. He was in eighth grade and I was in seventh. The crazy thing is, my mom was driving one of those busses, but not mine. I'll never forget him. He was a boy who was in my life just for a bus ride, but what a ride it was—thirty minutes of amazing lips.

I learned years later that Stony broke a lot of young girls' hearts. I do know he played football and wasn't in band in high school. I remember watching the team play; his dad was a really enthusiastic parent. One time the officials missed a call and Mr. Smithers stood up and screamed "Clipping! Clipping!" His false teeth flew out of his mouth and fell between the stands. Apparently, "Clipping" is similar to the mouth action required to remove dentures (are you sitting there trying it? I am!) He was such a great sport and laughed enthusiastically when he and a bunch of people exited the stands to run down and find them on the ground. I'm sure they were successful, because when I later saw him around town, he had his teeth.

As a freshman, I became part of marching band, and all the high school band kids came together in one class. It was seriously the best part of high school, and I highly recommend every parent encourage their kids to participate. It was hard work, but we learned discipline and teamwork. Band kids are absolutely good kids. Parents are always involved because it's a big group so there has to be a lot of chaperones (although I guess even a band geek might be able to kiss in the back of the bus if a parent isn't paying attention!).

On one trip, I rode with the Smittens home from an event. They had three boys—one was four years older than me. The oldest son was part of the group that came and taught us jazz band when I was in eighth grade, but he graduated before I got to high school. Their middle son, Robert, was two years older than me, and they had a younger son, John, who was a year younger than Heidi, so three years behind me. They were a really nice family.

Robert played the tuba. He was really smart. I seem to remember his adenoids blocked his nasal passages somewhat, so he always had his mouth open a bit all the time to allow him to breathe better. He had droopy Polish eyes and bowed legs like his sweet grandmother's. It was obviously hereditary because I never saw him ride horses all day which is what, at the time, I thought caused bowed legs.

After marching season was over, the ninth graders went back to their own band and the tenth to twelfth graders were in symphonic band. We got together for basketball games to be in the pep band. I loved the friendship I had found in this group of kids. After games, we'd go to Pizza Hut or McDonald's. I wasn't old enough to drive, but Robert's older brother still hung out with the band because band kids always stay friends, I guess. So he'd drive and I got to come along.

At some point, and I don't exactly know when, Robert asked me out. I asked Mom and Dad if I could go out with him, but Dad said Robert would have to come and ask permission himself if he wanted to take me out. Dad thought for sure that the fear of meeting him face-to-face would be the end of it, but I guess I was quite a catch (not!) because it didn't stop him. I turned fourteen the first week of my freshman year of high school; I was young to start dating, but like Mom said, I was more like an adult.

Robert borrowed his dad's green car and drove to our house. Let me explain that getting to our house from the road wasn't so easy. Mom and Dad found a ten-acre parcel of land in the country where Dad built our house. It was really a pretty spot—it had been part of pastureland Mr. Turcott used to graze his cows and horses. The location they chose to build the house was five acres back high up on the hill. Yes, it was a great place because we always had a breeze, but getting to the top sometimes was like the thrill of a car chase movie.

We had to start gunning the engine 150 feet down the road before the driveway started. Then, ever so slightly, we let up on the gas as we made the turn into the driveway. Remember, this was in the era of rear-wheel drive vehicles, so as we made the turn, the back end would swing out wildly to the right. It was a real talent to learn how much gas to give it so as not to lose speed in the sharp turn or risk the backend swinging around too far and accidentally hitting the waist-high very large tree stump that still stood proudly a couple of feet from the road. Once the correction to the backend was made, we'd push the accelerator to the floor—mashed it hard! We hit the first of two hills at high speed flying over it Dukes of Hazzard style as the large telephone pole whizzed past the right side of the car. It was not unusual at this point to hit our heads on the roof right before a brief flat spot where (hopefully) we got a little traction before we arrived at the Mt. Everest second precipice of total steepness—with trees on the left and a drop off with more trees close to the edge on the right. As the car slowed to an almost dead stop at the top due to the steep slope and loss of momentum, the wheels would spin futilely. It seemed that just as we said the last prayer of hope, the top wheels broke the crest of the hill. Remember, the front wheels aren't turning in a rear wheel drive car, so since they couldn't pull the back end up the rest of the way, all may be lost. But then, the back tires would grip some sparse gravel underneath the cool winter white and we were propelled forward to flat ground. We were home! We'd breathe deeply realizing we'd been holding our breath and grunting for the last thirty seconds at least. Similar to the thrill of a lamb birth, but a little different.

Scaling the driveway was fun—in the summer. In the winter, it was downright scary—especially because Heidi and I would make the whole adventure worse. Winters in Michigan used to be bad—I know everyone says that, but it was true.

Since Mom drove a school (or as she pronounced it, *skoo*) bus, she took Billy with her to work. It amazes me to think about it, but the school allowed him to ride on the little "countertop" to the left of her bus driver seat. No, we didn't have seat belts because I guess kids were disposable. Dad had left for work, so Heidi and I were entrusted to getting to the bus on our own.

We would watch out the front picture window toward the north where we could see the bus when it arrived at the bus stop before ours. It would stop at the crest of the hill, put on its flashers and that would be our clue to run full speed to the bottom of the hill. The hill was long! The driveway was full of ruts from the drama I just told you about. We were wearing unattractive snowmobile boots, so we were clodding and running at the same time. We'd bolt out the door screaming, "Runnn!"

Also know that Michigan is dark in the morning, so we were twisting ankles, running through the ruts—I'm surprised we lived… for this and the fact that Dad may kill us because…when there was lots of snow, there was the risk that we wouldn't make it to the bottom before the bus sped off (well, we could if we left *before* we saw the bus at the stop before ours, but there was hair to be done—who am I kidding—I showered every morning and my hair was wet and frozen stiff when I went to the bus stop, so basically I just didn't like to wake up on time—still don't!).

When the snow was deep, we resorted to extraordinary means to arrive on time—break out the toboggan! I'd get on the front, Heidi would get on behind me—she'd tuck her legs around me, I'd stuff my lunch bag in front of me and we'd push off having a really fast ride all the way to the bottom. If the snow on the driveway was good and greased up, we could actually get enough momentum to fly across the road and possibly slide under the bus, so sometimes we'd have to bail to the left and eat snow to stop our descent. Then, we'd ditch the toboggan to the side and get on the bus—like this was normal? Years later, Grace, our bus driver, told me she would get the biggest kick out of watching Heidi and I do this. If she saw us coming, she would wait until we arrived and clamor aboard panting and unable to see where to sit because of my fogged up glasses.

But Dad didn't see the humor because doing this caused the hill to become ice. When Dad had to get the tractor out to pull his truck or jeep up the second hill or out of the front yard after he got stuck, he'd ask us, "Did you girls ride the toboggan to the bus stop again?" Of course, we wouldn't look him in the eye as we innocently said, "No…" He really didn't know because we always got home from school and hid the toboggan back in the barn before he saw it. But, truly, parents do know everything.

After the "no" lie, we'd have to park at the bottom and carry groceries up with human leg power. In the spring, it was not unusual to find a lost can of tuna in the new grass sprouting from the recently frozen earth.

So this is what Robert had to endure to ask me on a date—the driveway. He made it. God's will or hot-blooded pursuit of a girl? I think the latter. I don't recall if he walked it or drove, but after he went through all the grief, Dad said he couldn't tell him no. So at fourteen, I was dating Robert, the tuba-playing, smart Pollock who was old enough to drive. He would be the one link in my paper chain of boyfriends. The good news was, I cared about another human. My heart softened, and I was a much nicer person. Even Billy didn't smell so bad.

CHAPTER 6

God Speaks

I got my first eight-hour-a-day, forty-hour-a-week job where Dad worked. Dad had been working there since I was in elementary school, and they were hiring employees' kids during the summer.

Living in Michigan, people love summer vacation because we have three months of beautiful weather, so hiring kids allowed the people in the factory to be off work and they could still keep the production lines running. They were paying $4.50/hour—way more than the $1/hour I made babysitting. I was stoked!

My job was to assemble the corrugated shipping boxes, hand stencil the outside of the case, and manually load the skid as the product came off the end of the line. Because I was only fifteen, I wasn't allowed to work on the production lines themselves. I also wasn't old enough to drive, so another employee's daughter would pick me up each day and drive me to work and back. I made enough money that summer to buy contact lenses. It's insane to think that I worked for six weeks to buy them! Vanity has a steep price.

I loved my job! The people were really nice and the time went so fast. The only bad part was the vitamins smelled really bad, so when I left work, I had to take a shower as soon as I got home. But the paycheck made it worth everything!

I have always loved reading, and to this day, when I go on vacation from life, my suitcase usually contains at least five books. A good vacation is measured by whether I complete a three-hundred-page book each day. I started my love of reading young. In middle school, many summers were spent going to the library and hurrying home to admire the covers and decide which one I would read first. I read multiple books each day; five was the goal. It's miraculous that I didn't weigh a huge amount considering the negative calories I probably burned. I rarely moved in my bed except to turn the page or shift the book from one hand to another as the hand holding the book became cold from lack of blood flow.

The stories of choice in my early teens were Harlequin Romance novels. They were short, so finishing a few each day was possible which fed my overachieving need to finish what I started. The main drive was to get to the end of the book because they kissed and I knew that all the anguish they'd gone through was over and they lived happily ever after…thus, the lack of necessity for the story to extend past the kiss; the drama in their lives was over.

Yes, I'm fully aware that life after the first kiss for my parents wasn't always happily ever after (Oh wait, my parents kissed? Disgusting!), but it didn't stop me from thinking that everyone except my parents had a happily ever after. Therefore, I wasn't really prepared for the full-face smack of reality that was soon to hit me.

Because I was a really fast typist and could take shorthand (that I never truly used for employment, but it was really handy for taking notes in school when I didn't want the person beside me in class to be able to read what I was writing), I got a co-op job as a clerk in our local law firm, Bartl, Haslett, Baugh, and Laudenslater. It was fun answering the phone and saying their names fast, but not so fun having to type their names on every piece of correspondence. My job primarily was filing pages in legal books and making copies of documents. I really loved it mostly, because I was able to work with two impressive legal secretaries who seemed on the ball, and Char, who I guess I would say was my boss, treated me like an adult. Looking back, I'm not sure that any of the papers I filed ever ended up in the right book, but maybe they did.

Anyway, Char seemed quite old to me—I think she probably was only in her thirties, but that was twice my age. She had an elementary-age son and she was getting married. I guess I never really thought about the reality that she had been in a relationship before if she had a son and I was really focused on this marriage thing. Remember, Harlequin Romance novels were my number one interest.

I remember one afternoon asking Char, "Is he the one?"

She looked at me and matter-of-fact replied, "He'd better be. He's the third one!"

One thing my parents did teach me is manners. Dad gave us eating lessons at the table and although I didn't always appreciate them at the time, nor did I question how my dad, who was raised on a farm knew so much about etiquette, but we were very well behaved. So, when Char said this to me, *on the inside* I gasped *loudly*, but I don't remember replying verbally to her other than, "Oh."

But it's the other thing that happened on my inside that I'll ever forget. In the loudest booming voice ever to resound within myself, I heard God say, "Do not judge her, you too will be married three times!"

It knocked me flat—not physically, of course, but emotionally. At sixteen years old, I didn't talk or think like that for one, *and* there was no doubt it was God speaking.

Another thing that made an impact on me was Char being married three times. I respected her. I liked her. She was kind to me. I felt like she was a really good mother to her son. She was patient and taught me things…sometimes taking time to explain the same things to me over and over. She was a really good lady. Can good ladies be married three times? Perhaps. I didn't judge her and I knew I would one day be married three times, too.

The odd thing was, I wasn't scared. I wasn't upset. But it was a fact. I really wanted God to be wrong, but in the depths of my soul, I knew He was speaking to my heart and I was going to heed His words. The words I heard were not of my imagination. God's voice wasn't mean, but firm. He knew what I was thinking and He was going to put a stop to it and He did. It was like a swift verbal swat from my dad when I was getting rowdy in public when I was supposed to behave, "Settle down!" With my eyes looking down and my emotions in check, I moved on with the rest of my day—never to forget the words He first spoke to me—the foresight into my future. I, too, would be married three times.

CHAPTER 7

Dad, Does God Really Forgive Everything?

Having a best friend was fun. I always knew that I had someone to do things with, but having a boyfriend caused conflict for me.

Robert was studious. There are certainly worse characteristics to have in a boyfriend! We spent a lot of time together doing our homework. I was a good student—not as good as Robert; I finished thirteenth out of my class of 205; he finished first in his. I am thankful that education was a priority for him because schoolwork came first and there are no regrets about that.

However, besides band, there was little fun. I started dating Robert my freshman year. Before I went out with him, I went to one high school dance. I never went to another dance until his prom. We didn't fit in at prom because we weren't party kids. When others went out afterward/during to sneak a drink, we sat at the table with our other band friends.

After feeling out of place at prom, "we" decided that it wasn't worth the money to get dressed up and go to prom or dances, so we just didn't go. Was I disappointed? Yes, but I didn't ever stick up for myself. I didn't want to deny him anything, so I went along with what he said. I didn't disagree or argue. That wouldn't be nice.

Neither one of our families were wealthy, but our parents worked hard and we had love. Vacations to Disney were for rich people. I remember telling Billy that he couldn't ask for new shoes when his didn't fit. I told him Mom and Dad couldn't afford new shoes. His shoes didn't fit, but he didn't ask because I wouldn't let him. Years later, I told Mom I did that to him and she was horrified—we were never that poor, but in my mind...

Dad was an accountant and he showed me how to budget and how to write checks. He taught me to be careful, but my over-crazy about not spending anything to the point of extreme came from Robert.

Robert was Catholic. His dad played the organ at church and I adored him! We shared a love for the keyboards. He was so welcoming to me and often he would let me sit on the organ bench and try to play with my feet. I could never do it, but he sure could!

Things were different at the Smittens'. His mom had dessert after dinner every night. We had dessert only when there was company. Dessert was for the "real people" (guests), so I guess we weren't real people at home, but I was at the Smittens'.

Also different—I could go into Robert's bedroom, but he shared his room with his older brother, so it's not like we were alone. Robert was not allowed in my room. Unfortunately, rules about being in bedrooms or not, that is not the only place to be intimate. Robert had his dad's car and on the way to take me home, he would pull over on a dirt road to park. Unfortunately, when I was sixteen years old, I gave up my virginity to him.

I was devastated. My faith in God and my desire to live a Christian life was so strong. I was sure that I had done something God could never forgive. I was scared. I wasn't on birth control. In my whole life, besides the risk of my mom and dad's marriage dissolving, this was the most terrible thing I had encountered.

*****

As much as my dad was a quiet person when he was at home, when I was disciplined, my dad is the one who would come to my room to talk about it afterward—to put me back together. I remember one of our talks and I asked, "Dad, can God really forgive everything?" He told me yes, but I was sure Dad was wrong and sex outside of marriage was unforgiveable. My guilt was huge!

When I was young in my Christian walk, I could not comprehend grace—complete forgiveness that I cannot earn—for anything except denying him. I thought the rules that God inflicted on us were just to make sure we never had fun; now I understand there is nothing further from the truth—he is protecting us from the nastiness of our world, from Satan's temptations that will hurt us and drive us further from Him, and from ramifications of bad choices that make our lives harder. He tries to protect us from Satan's lure so life can be more rich and fun. Satan lies.

There is a really messed up thought that we women have that men can fix us and complete us. Whatever! Let me say that again, "Whatever!" The only man we need and the only man who will complete us is Jesus. Read that sentence again!

A man is a man and we are a woman. We have no superpowers other than the power God puts within us. We are God's creation. When we think that a man can make us whole, we put ridiculous pressure on the man to be something he can never be.

Now, to clarify, God says in Genesis 1:26, "Then God said, 'Let *us* make man in *our* image, in *our* likeness, and let them rule over the fish of the sea and the birds of the air, over the livestock, over all the earth, and over all the creatures that move along the ground.' So God created man in His *own* image, in the image of God He created him; male and female He created them. God blessed them and said to them, 'Be fruitful and increase in number; fill the earth and subdue it. Rule over the fish of the sea and the birds of the air and over every living creature that moves on the ground.'"

So we have dominion over things of the earth. We are definitely quite incredible, but we are not gods and men are not gods. Men can't fix everything for us. Hopefully a handy guy can fix a leak in the sink, build homes, put together gas grills and not blow up the house, but they can't complete our hearts, our souls, our being…that is only for God to do—for the Holy Spirit to do—only He can fill us.

But as a teenage (or any age girl), I was looking for fulfillment from my man. I was willing to forgo my own wishes to make Robert happy so that he would like me. That's just stupid! (Grandma Van hated that word *stupid*, so sorry, Gram.)

I thought I had boundaries. I didn't want to have sex before marriage because God said I shouldn't. Why? Because God says in Genesis 1:24 we will leave our father and mother and be united and will become one flesh. I hadn't left my father and mother; I was still part of my family; it was not time to become one flesh, but I physically become one flesh with Robert and there the problems began.

Guilt... I had it. I didn't tell dad what I thought God couldn't forgive. I'm not sure if he knew, but to me, I had done the biggest no-no of my life. If I had only understood—then and there—that God came to save me *no matter what* because He loves me completely. He loves me so much that He stretched out His arms and when I asked, "How much do You love me?" He stretched out His arms wide and said, "This big!" and then my sin nailed those arms to the cross and He died for me to wipe me clean. When I stand before the Father in heaven on judgment day, Jesus stands in front of me. He takes my sin upon Himself and I am free.

How can someone love that much? It's beyond my comprehension, but it's real. All I needed to do was confess my sin. Repent. Christ says in Luke 24:46–47, "He told them, 'This is what is written: The Christ will suffer and rise from the dead on the third day, and repentance and forgiveness of sins will be preached in his name to all nations.'" Christ did suffer, He rose, and He forgave my sins— all of them—even the biggie of sex before marriage. He said it, but I didn't believe it...not yet.

Even though I carried guilt, my desire to not lose Robert was stronger than my guilt. We continued to have sex. Did I even tell him I didn't want to do this? I don't think so.

Someone once told me, "Girls play at sex to get love. Boys play at love to get sex." It's true. I know that we are made to leave our parents and be with a man, but there is a time for such things and the drive within us is so amazingly strong and Satan makes it seem so wonderful...more wonderful than using our brain and waiting for His perfect plan. Satan sucks!

Pleasing my parents was also huge for me. As much as I loved them and as much as they never put me down, this failure/decision on my part was so horrible that I wouldn't tell them that I was sexually active. I'm sure my parents wouldn't have disowned me and they would have still loved me, and I'm confident my mother would have understood and probably would have taken me to the doctor to get birth control. But she wouldn't know to do that with my mouth shut tightly about my sin. Instead, I just lived scared. I was just living stupid!

I was sure I was going to marry him because I had to—I needed to make it right with God. I had this crazy idea in my head that if I married Robert, it would somehow erase my sin. Yeah, that's biblical—not! By this time, I'd read the Bible three times through, so the stupid Satan lies I was believing just amaze me. All I had to do was confess my sin and let God take it, but I was holding on to it tightly—sealing it away in a dirty little place in my heart.

One afternoon, we stopped at the Gun River Conservation Club, which was on the way to my house. No one was there, and we never had gone there to park before (or after). When he turned off the car, one of us jokingly made a comment that we never got in the back seat. *Happy Days* was one of our favorite TV shows, and they were always going parking in the back seat. Robert now had his own 1968 Ford Mustang and the back seat was small, so it wasn't like it would be that comfortable, but as we laughed about the whole thought of it, we said, "Okay!"

We went through the cumbersome process of climbing in the back seat and then shutting the doors again—it wasn't so easy. The end result was we were trapped back there in this tiny little space. We were doing absolutely nothing except laughing about back seats being a rather dumb idea when a police officer drove up. I thought I would die. As if I didn't have enough guilt, now in broad daylight, an officer was finding me in the back seat with a boy. I also was a minor and Robert was not. So I was scared out of my mind! We were fully clothed, but we were not supposed to be there.

The officer came up to the window and asked what we were doing. We said we were just talking. It was true! He asked us, "In the back seat?"

Oh my gosh! We didn't lie to him and I was just thankful that we weren't doing anything else. He asked us if more people were with us and we told him no. He explained that they had some break-ins, so he needed to take our names and contact information. He said if nothing ended up missing or broken into, he wouldn't contact us and there's be no further action, but I was so upset. I was supposed to be a good girl, and now the police had my information. *Scared to death!*

We never heard anything further, but we never got in the back of a car to make out again and most certainly, we never went parking at the Gun River Conservation Club.

Honestly, what thrill is there is making out in a car? Maybe I'm weird, okay, I am weird, but I don't think sex is great enough to do it in the car anyway! I guess if I was a guy, I'd probably think differently or we wouldn't have been there in the first place!

*****

Robert and I had a thing we did—we saved every quarter. We were going to use it to buy a water bed when we got married. Oh yes, water beds were a thing. Even if we bought something for ten cents, we would save the three quarters we got with the change. The teachers at school knew we were saving quarters and one time, one of our math teachers threw a quarter down the hall to us. It makes me smile. We were really good kids. We loved and respected our teachers very much and I know they enjoyed us too.

Bottom line, I felt my future was mapped out for me. I wasn't going to be able to go out with any other guy. At sixteen, my future was determined because of my sin. There would be no dances at school. No going out with friends. Just studying and planning for being an adult.

Robert graduated and went on to Western Michigan University to study teaching and math. Since he was two years ahead of me, at least one day a week, he would meet me in front of the school at lunchtime. He'd go to McDonald's and get me a Filet-O-Fish sandwich and I'd sit in his car and we'd eat our lunch. The vice principal of the high school, master of all discipline, and darn right scary guy, would sometimes come out to the car. He'd cross his arms on his chest and give us an evil side-eye. He'd look in the windows checking out inside our car like we were hiding something. He freaked me out. Of course, we were never doing anything except eating our lunch and talking, but it was like he knew I was a bad girl.

When I was a senior, the worst thing I could imagine happened. I was late. Not for lunch, not for church, not for work, not late period, but period late. Since we essentially used no reliable birth control (and I knew better because my biology paper was entitled "Pregnancy"), I was very good about worrying about my next period. My period was my true friend.

I knew it—I was definitely late. One day, two days...fourteen days. It was time to tell Mom.

I told her I thought I was pregnant. She cried. The thing is, she wasn't crying because she was disappointed in me. She wasn't crying because she was mad at me. She was crying because she knew I had plans to go to college and have a career and being pregnant meant I would set all that aside. I was responsible. She knew I'd raise the baby—my life would be harder. She wanted my dreams for me and they were crashing down around me—all because of stupid boy choices. I calculated I could finish high school before I had the baby, but college was out of the question.

She said, "Well, we'll take a pregnancy test." She didn't scold me. She didn't yell at me. She wiped her tears and went to the store.

That night, she explained how it worked. We had to put urine in these little containers and we let them set overnight. I remember putting them behind the shower curtain on the tub ledge—sealing them in their secret place until morning.

The next day, I woke up, went into the bathroom and pulled back the shower curtain. With huge fear, I looked into the little containers and the results were negative. I wasn't pregnant. I was never so relieved. But why was I late? I was one of those weird girls who had been having twenty-eight-day cycles since I was ten—for six years, I was menstruating like clockwork. What was happening?

The following day, I started my period. Sigh—the biggest sigh of my entire life!

Mom made an appointment with the doctor and she told me that the stress of worrying if I was pregnant was likely the reason I hadn't had my period.

She didn't need to put me on birth control because I told Robert that I wasn't having sex with him anymore until we were married. I was not having a baby out of wedlock. What we did was dirty and it was wrong. He understood.

To show you what a good guy he was, he didn't argue about my decision.

I still had to make my sin go away by marrying him (I thought!), but the pressure of being pregnant was gone for now. I could enjoy being his friend.

I suggested to my best friend that she should date Robert. She looked at me oddly and said, "But he's your boyfriend!" But I didn't want him to be, but I wouldn't be mean and break up with him. I wanted him just for a platonic friend, but I held that inside.

*****

I graduated from high school in 1981. I was going to Kalamazoo Valley Community College to study nursing in the fall.

My curfew was still 11:00 p.m. even though I was in college! I was still living at home, but my parents never changed my curfew time. Years later, when I was at Mom and Dad's and Billy wasn't home at eleven fifteen, I was freaking out—why wasn't he home? Mom said, "His curfew is midnight." What? I asked them why my curfew was eleven until I got married. Mom and Dad looked at each other and smirked—"you never asked!"

Not only was my curfew eleven, we were not supposed to be at each other's house alone. Not that it didn't happen, but it was rare. So I knew something was up when we were at Robert's house and he was going to make me dinner and his parents weren't there. Not only weren't they there, they had been, and they left—leaving us alone. Weird.

Robert made little steaks, and when we were done eating, I went to their entryway to put my shoes on so he could take me home, and he got down on one knee and asked me to marry him. We had shopped for rings together, but he had bought the ring by himself without my knowledge. I can't say I was surprised, but he was very sweet about it. My ring was tiny, but so were my hands. The diamonds were sparkly. Of course, I said yes. I was going to make my sins go away.

We planned our wedding for August the next year. I enthusiastically got a wedding checklist and starting going through all my tasks with great discipline because that's how I am! My dress was from the JC Penney catalog and cost me $109. I tried it on for everyone I could—Mom said I had the most tried on wedding dress ever. It had long sleeves even though I was going to get married in August, but I bought it anyway because it was the least expensive.

*****

I planned to go back to work the summer after graduation. The company was really small back then and there was a guy in human resources, Louie Johnston, who everyone knew was the fastest typist typing 85 wpm on a Selectric II electric typewriter, but Dad knew I could beat him and dad told him so.

Louie's interest was piqued, and he told Dad to bring me in. I was horribly shy, but I loved to type. So, when Dad told me I was going for the test, I was scared to death, but really excited—I mean, what if I could beat Louie? Dad said I could. Louie and I didn't have side-by-side typewriters, but he did set me up with a manual typing test and I skunked him typing 103 wpm with no errors.

Louie wasn't mad. He was in awe and told me if I could type that fast, I wasn't going back to the plant to work; he was going to have me be a typist for Charlie Cabot, the chief chemist. It seemed Charlie had file cabinets filled with handwritten test methods and he wanted them all typed. (I think about the fact that years later, someone had to do it all again to put them into a computer, but we didn't have computers yet!—I'm so old!)

The first day working for Charlie, I was to meet him in the human resources office across the street. Dad and I could now ride together to work because we worked eight to five. Dad's always late. I mean always! So at 8:03 a.m., Charlie left and went back to his office. At 8:05 a.m., Dad and I showed up at human resources, and Louie told us Charlie had been there and was gone. Dad walked me to Charlie's office. Charlie took one look at me and said, "You're late." Gulp! What Louie hadn't told me is that Charlie was a grumpy old man. I was scared.

Another twist is that there was no real place for me to type. Charlie had arranged to have a typewriter put in his office on a tiny table just large enough to hold my blue typewriter and a piece of paper. It is there that I sat and typed all summer long. Charlie faced away from me toward the window and I faced the rows of filing cabinets...typing one page at a time...day after day for weeks.

Charlie rarely spoke unless people came into his office to ask him a question—after all, he was the *chief* chemist, the big boss of the laboratory. But after a few weeks, I guess Charlie's heart started to soften toward me. I worked hard and I was fast. One day, I felt a rubber band whiz over and hit me. Looking back at Charlie, he was facing the windows like nothing happened. I smiled. I think he liked me.

One day when Charlie was not in his office, one of the other chemists came in and told me, "You know, I'm sorry Charlie is grouchy. He has bone cancer and he doesn't always feel well."

I learned a lesson that day. We don't always know why people are the way they are, but there is a person inside every human body—a unique person who is made by God. When God says not to judge, it's because we don't know what's happening with them. We don't know their story. If we did, we may think differently about them. We shouldn't assume. That day, I understood a little more about Charlie. I loved Charlie a lot more. He was going through something tough, and I needed to be understanding and kind. I didn't have cancer. I wasn't dying. Charlie was dying. I could be just a little bit nicer and work a little harder and make Charlie's life just a smidge better.

Charlie and I never spoke of his cancer. But I took a lot more rubber band hits over the summer. At the end of my time with dear Charlie, he gave me a card with a $50 bill inside. He told me he wanted me to buy a college textbook with the money. He told me he knew college books were expensive and he wanted to help me out.

It meant so much to me! I am crying as I write this because he touched me so very deeply. This man cared for me and I had fallen in love with this old grumpy codger and I was going to miss him something fierce…and I still do!

When I got to college that fall, the most expensive textbook I had was my anatomy/physiology book. It was thick and I would use it for two semesters. Charlie paid for that book and I thought of him every time I opened it. I aced those classes—for Charlie!

Charlie did end up dying of bone cancer—he worked a few more years. A number of years later, I was volunteering at the 4-H food booth at the county fair, and I was introduced to another volunteer. Her last name was Mrs. Cabot. I asked her if she knew Charlie. She told me, "He was my husband." I told her the story about Charlie and me. She was very moved. She never knew he gave me that money, but it warmed her heart that I had treasured him and he had done this nice thing for me.

"Finally, all of you, live in harmony with one another; be sympathetic, love as brothers, be compassionate and humble. Do not repay evil with evil or insult with insult, but with blessing, because to this you were called so that you may inherit a blessing" (1 Pet. 3:8–9).

I inherited a blessing. I did the right thing in how I treated Charlie—I loved on him, and my time with him has blessed me my whole life, not just with the $50 for my text book but the dear memories I have of my summer typing for Charlie. I hope I see Charlie in heaven and tell him how much he meant to me.

*****

I finished my first year of college and completed all my nursing prerequisites. Robert completed his third year of college, and in the fall, he would start student teaching.

We arranged for an apartment in Kalamazoo—the absolutely cheapest one-bedroom apartment we could find. We would move in after we got married.

We planned our honeymoon to Oahu, Hawaii. It would be my first airplane ride and my first venture outside of Michigan and the states that border it.

We started premarital counseling with Father Martin at the Catholic church Robert and his family attended. We went to all the classes, and at the completion, we had to sign a paper saying we would raise our children in the Catholic Church. We looked at each other hesitantly and signed the paper. After we left, I looked at him and said, "I don't think I want to raise our children in the Catholic Church." He said, "I don't either."

Robert would often come with me to the Lutheran church and we both wanted to be Lutheran, but what were we going to do? More guilt. His family was so faithful—Mr. Smitten played the organ for services. We called Father Martin and asked to talk to him face-to-face.

When we told him our concerns, he was amazing. He told us he didn't care if we raised them in the Catholic Church or the Lutheran church—what was most important is that we raised them in the Christian church and whichever one we chose didn't matter.

So at our wedding, we had both Father Martin and Pastor Dennis Nichols officiate. Both families were happy.

The challenge was location. Hope Lutheran Church was meeting in the Plainwell Middle School cafeteria. I really didn't want to get married in the cafeteria. I had a dream of walking down a long aisle. Mom said the longest aisle she knew was at Zion Lutheran in Kalamazoo. Since we didn't have a building, Zion opened their doors and I was able to travel down that longest aisle. That day, I married my best friend.

They threw bird seed at us when we came out of the church because I'd heard that rice will hurt birds when they swallow it.

The wedding reception was at St. Margaret's school cafeteria (I guess there was going to be a cafeteria in there somewhere). It was blistering hot and there was no air. I wore my inexpensive long-sleeved dress and felt near death from heat stroke. When I finally was able to sit down to my meal, behind the white cloth draping around the head table, I pulled my long dress up over my legs as high as it would go and whispered to Robert, "I have my dress pulled up high on my legs. It feels better this way." Little did I know that they were recording the wedding and reception and there was a microphone right by me. Later, when family got together with us to watch it, I had to hear what sounded like a torrid movie line coming out of my mouth. After I explained that he wasn't doing anything inappropriate to me under the table, it was quite hysterical!

We went back to our apartment together for the first time after the reception. I took off my dress and found hundreds of pieces of bird seed imbedded deeply into my sweaty skin!

It was going to be the first day making love in a year and a half. For Robert, it had been a long wait. For me, the reality was that I was going to have to do the dirty, wrong thing again. I told Robert I was really tired—could we just wait until tomorrow. He politely said yes. How sad for him.

Making my decision to marry him when I didn't have feelings for him as a wife should for a husband—because of sin and guilt—it was so wrong. In my dumb mind, I was fixing things, but I was really hurting this nice man. Yes, he took my virginity—he owns that. But if only I had said no. A girl has a choice! I could have faced my failure and given it to God to heal me, but I did none of those things— instead, I kept moving ahead with the lie in my heart.

We left the next morning for Chicago and boarded my first airplane. We landed in Oahu, went to our small, cockroach-filled hotel room. We found the least expensive restaurants we could find—buffets! I gained ten pounds that week—literally! We had fun doing as many free things as we could.

Two things I won't forget. Snorkeling! We were picked up by a guy in a van who took us to Hanauma Bay. He gave us snorkel equipment and we were able to stay on the beach all day. It had been raining the day before, so the water wasn't clear. I was petrified to go into the water. This was the era of Jaws! I knew what was in the ocean. Finally, after Robert had been swimming around for hours, he convinced me to come into the water. I held on so tightly to his hand and he pointed out a piece of coral to me. I thought it was an immense fish coming to eat me (I mean, it was cloudy). I pushed him hard as I started thrashing, which caused him to swallow a bunch of water and I swam/ran back to the safety of my towel where I spent the rest of the day.

On the van trip to the bay, the driver pointed out the road that led to Tom Selleck's house. Oh my gosh! I was all about Tom—Magnum PI—he was my #1 hunk!

Later, we took a rental car and drove to the road the driver had pointed out to us. We followed his instructions driving to the end and saw the gray house he had described. We knew it had to be his house because there was a Detroit Tiger ball cap visible on the window ledge. The gate to his backyard was open and I ran from the car, through the gate, and stole a hibiscus flower from the bush in his yard. I ran as fast as I could back to the car with Robert yelling at me for doing it. I didn't care, but I felt like I was going to get arrested as if I'd robbed a bank and stole a million dollars. I took the flower home and pressed it in a paper towel inside a book. After it dried, I framed it and had it hanging on my wall for years. I know stealing is a sin, but it's one I managed to survive with great excitement!

After a few days, I wanted to go home. I had never been away from my parents in my life. I was only eighteen years old and I was expected to be a wife and a woman. At the end of our week in paradise, I was happy to leave—so sad.

*****

We got home and settled into our apartment. A few weeks later, we were back in school. I was starting my nursing rotation. I loved the science of nursing; I loved learning period!

My first rotation was in the nursing home. All my grandparents were still living and I loved them so much. Here I was faced with people their age that were not doing well. They had no one who visited them. They were loaded into their wheelchairs and placed in the hall to stare at the walls. It was a place I thought that was close to hell on earth.

One man asked me to comb his hair. I did my best, but he yelled at me, "Don't you know how to comb a man's hair?" No, I really didn't. I was petrified of him, but I remembered Charlie; there must be a reason he was grumpy. I made conversation with him as much as I could, and he started to soften. I found out from the staff that he hadn't had a visitor since he'd been there—over three years. I asked him if he ever went outside. Never. I asked him if he'd like that and he said yes.

I went to his cupboard and found he only had pajamas. The dear man had no clothes to wear outside. No worries. I just put a blanket on his lap and we headed for the front door. I pushed him down the sidewalk. It was a beautiful sunny day. When we got to the end of the block, I wheeled him around and we went back the other way, past the nursing home to the other end of the block. Then he told me he thought we should get back. We had probably been gone five minutes, but it was the first five minutes outside of the building he'd had in all that time.

I took him out other times after that. His heart softened and he never yelled at me anymore for not combing his hair right. I will never forget him either. He taught me something else. When I give to someone, I get a bigger gift in return. I am the one blessed. Since that time, my biggest joy has been to give; it returns the biggest interest for my heart.

My time at the nursing home was really hard. My heart was so tender and it was breaking with every patient.

I talked to my nursing instructor and I told her I couldn't do this—I couldn't be a nurse. I told her why. She reassured me that after this rotation, I wouldn't be in the nursing home any more—I would move to the hospital. Just hang in a little longer. I did. Rotations were only nine weeks long.

At the end of the rotation, we found out where we were moving next and with dread I looked at the list and it said I was going back to the nursing home. I went to the head of the nursing program and asked her why. She explained that there were three of us who were going back to the nursing home because there was not room in the other rotation spots for us. I told her I couldn't do it and why. She told me, "I think your heart hurts because you care and I think you should major in geriatrics." Was she kidding? No! I politely told her I was going to quit the program. I just couldn't do it. She was very sad. She told me I was the top student in the program and if at any time in the future I wanted to reenter, she would place me immediately.

It was so hard—I had never quit anything before in my life, but I couldn't continue; I was miserable. My heart was too tender to witness the sadness I saw every day.

*****

Since I liked working in the office so much, I called my friend Louie and asked him if he had something I could do until the next semester started. I was going to switch my major to business.

Louie told me that there was a temporary typist position in the sales organization and I could have it if I wanted it. Yes!

I met Gia; she would be my boss for the next few weeks. I loved her! She was bubbly and kind. I enjoyed working for her so much. After one week, Gia asked me if I would like to work there permanently. She offered me $5.50 per hour and they would pay for my college. It would mean that I would need to go to school at night, but it would be free and I would be rich.

Robert and I talked it over and it would mean that I could put him through school his last year and we would have fewer financial worries. I took the full-time job and the next semester, I started my education in business. I went to work Monday through Friday and Monday through Thursday, I left work and went to college.

When Robert graduated with his teaching degree, I was so excited because he got a full-time job making $12,500/year, which was the same amount I made, so I could now go to school full-time while he worked. He told me no; I had to keep working full-time going to school part-time and we would save one of our checks for a house. It made sense. I liked my job. I'll admit, I was tired. I spent the weekends doing homework and I had no time to enjoy life, but we were saving for our house and interest rates were 16.5 percent, so every dollar we saved was growing.

CHAPTER 8

A Career Woman

When Dad started working for his employer, it was really no place for a woman. I don't know that Dad was really happy that I was working there full-time; it still was no place for a woman. Women were allowed to have entry-level management positions, but leadership positions were reserved for men—men over six feet tall—not women five-foot, three-and-three-fourth-inches tall.

Gia was wonderful! She treated me like a friend and a person, but when guys made rude comments to me, I had to learn to deal with it because the guys thought it was funny.

I remember a time one of the sales guys was on the phone with his customer and I walked in to his cubicle. He said to the customer, "Can you hold on a second? My secretary just came in and she needs to sit on my face." He laughed. I was horrified; I turned and walked out. He never apologized, but I had dreams at night that I would pinch his neck so hard that his head would pop off and float away like a balloon.

Another time, a customer from New York was talking to me on the phone, and he told me he just wanted to see me naked on a bear skin rug. I think I just ignored him, finished our business, and hung up. I told the sales director who managed the account that his customer made me feel very uncomfortable. He told me, "Diane, he's the customer. Just put up with it if it makes him happy."

I had to write a paper for one of my college classes about women in business. I actually interviewed one of the sales directors and they told me that a woman should not be allowed to be in sales because she wouldn't be able to carry her luggage and if it was bad weather and her hair got messy, she wouldn't be able to go on the call. He really truly believed it—he wasn't just being funny. I got an A on my paper. Later, when I was in sales, I never forgot his opinion. I was glad he was wrong—I could heft my own luggage and my hair was never a problem. Unreal! I'm so thankful things have changed!

One of the other administrative assistants and I would talk about the men when they were at lunch. She asked me, "If you had to sleep with one of them to get ahead, which one would you choose?" We both decided that we'd rather not get ahead because we didn't want to sleep with any of them!

Gia was promoted to a job in customer service and a new lady was brought in to be our boss. Jan was new to the company. When she saw how the men treated us, she asked about it. I told her they thought it was funny. She asked me if I thought it was funny and I told her, "No!"

She went and talked to the men and told them it had better not happen again. She told me they felt badly; I don't know if they did or not, but they did know that we had someone who wouldn't tolerate their poor behavior and it did stop. Culture was changing!

I got promoted every year, and within a couple of years, I was offered a management job. I couldn't believe it! I was so happy. I loved the people I worked with and who worked for me.

I graduated magna cum laude from Kalamazoo Valley with my associate's degree in business, and I was being rewarded at work. I started my bachelor's program at Western Michigan University.

I continued to move up in management. I had four different management jobs in a short amount of time. I didn't have to apply to any of them; the managers in those areas asked me if I wanted the position. It felt good to be recognized, but most important is that I was learning and I loved it!

CHAPTER 9

Physical Labor

When Dad built our house as kids, I was fascinated watching. He showed me there was nothing he couldn't do; he just did it.

My parents sold our house in Comstock and we moved to Plainwell the summer between fourth and fifth grades. I never thought about the insanity of selling a house and having nowhere to go, but they had a plan.

Grandpa and Grandma Van had a relatively small camper that had a small kitchen with a fold-down table that converted into a bed and a very tiny sitting area. They hauled the camper to our new home, and it sat right at the top of the crazy, insane driveway.

Grandpa Van also had a big army tent, and that was erected in the yard. Many of our boxed-up possessions were put in the tent as well as a Porta Potty.

A second smaller tent was erected that would be the bedroom. All our box springs and mattresses were stacked into two piles—one on each side of the doorway. Mom, Dad, and Billy slept on the top of one pile, and Heidi and I slept on top of the other pile.

What more could we need? Oh a bath? Once a week, Mom took us to town to Barbara and Bill Burr's house for a bath. That's all we needed for sure!

I don't really remember how Dad worked and completed what he did that summer, but I know my two grandpas helped some too.

Grandpa Van was a teacher/superintendent/principal, so he had summers off. I was surrounded by some handy Get'er Done Guys!

Dad hired someone to put in the driveway, dig out the hillside for the basement, and put the cement block walls on the three sides that were in the hill. Everything else, he finished himself with help from the grandpas.

I'll never forget the next step—pouring the basement floor. I don't remember why, but instead of having the cement truck pull in front of the house where there was no wall, they unloaded it from the back of the house over the back wall. The guy didn't have a long enough shoot, and the cement essentially fell eight feet from the truck's short shoot to its final resting place on the basement floor. The weight, volume, and speed of the cement caused an eruption of cement flying everywhere and probably resulted in a very deep pit of cement where it hit—maybe it's where they laid Jimmy Hoffa.

The guys were wearing heavy rubber boots—I think Dad's boots were the ones he wore as a volunteer fireman when I was very little. Grandpa Koehl's face was pocked with small circles of cement that had landed and dried on his face. As the cement continued to cascade to the floor, the guys moved the two-by-four board on edge back and forth across the surface trying to smooth it out using their boots to kick from behind to fill in any gaps that were left in this leveling process. I watched every step—worrying every second.

People say if you are worrying, you're not praying, and if you're praying, you're not worrying. Since a small age, I have been a good multitasker and when there is cement involved, I can multitask really hard!

Once the cement floor was done, I watched Dad frame the front of the house, and then they brought in a giant I-beam that was lowered in place in the center of the house that would support all of the floor joists. I did some more multitask worrying watching that big beam. It amazed me how flexible it was from side to side, but Dad explained to me that once it was in place on the wall, the steel beam could hold huge amounts of pressure from on top with no bend. In my mind, I could understand the physics of it, even though I was only ten years old. I was fascinated! Dad supported the big I-beam using posts beneath it every few feet.

Then came the floor joists and then the subfloor and the "dance floor" was done. Dad added a big blue tarp, and we had a roof on our basement. That roof would become the floor to the main level of the house, but Mom and Dad finished the house as they had money. For now, we had a structure that could be closed in where we could live.

Job one was hooking up a toilet. It was in the center of the basement. Dad hung blankets around the four sides so we had some privacy. Later, we had a kiddy pool for a bathtub! There couldn't be anything more fun as a kid than all this!

We had rock stores (okay, no one bought them, but we collected them and pretended). Being a kid was amazing and I watched, learned, and remembered—I remembered how this building stuff worked and I learned that there is nothing you can't do if you know how.

Once Robert and I had enough quarters (and dollars) saved, we bought not only our water bed, but eventually a seven-acre piece of property. We talked to Mr. Doster from Doster Lumber, and we told him how much money we had for materials. He agreed to sell us whatever materials we needed for the house and when we ran out of money, he would give us credit for the rest on the condition that we bought everything from him. Deal!

We sketched out what we wanted on a piece of paper and called in reinforcements to help. My cousin Anne's husband was a cement guy, so he did the floor (no more doing that ourselves—I learned that lesson from the cement splotches on Grandpa Koehl's face). We found a framer who said he could just frame the house from our rustic drawing and he did.

Grandpa Koehl and Dad did the wiring. Grandpa taught me how to do it—asking the important question, "Is the power off?" and I answered "Yes!" and he got zapped. He said, "I thought the power was off." I looked sadly at him and said, "Sorry, Grandpa, I thought it was!" Thankfully he loved me and didn't die. Then I turned the breaker off and he kept teaching me how to wire and ground a plug.

The back of the house was brick. Dad laid the brick showing me what to do. When he wasn't there, I'd work on it myself. I loved it! Dad didn't dismiss my curiosity. He taught me. He believed in me. Because he believed I could do it, I believed I could do it, and I did.

This belief in my own potential was huge for me as a person and later as a leader!

Grandma June Koehl was not a typical woman from her generation. During WWII, when the men were fighting, Grandma went to work in the factory as a welder. When the men came back from war, Grandma kept working because she enjoyed it.

What frustrated her is they wouldn't let her be a manager because she was a woman. Over the years, she trained man after man how to do the job they wouldn't allow her to do. She was smart. She was inquisitive, and if she believed she could do something, she did.

She and Grandpa Koehl built their A-frame house. Grandma wanted a fieldstone fireplace that would go all the way from the basement through the top of the house—over three stories of stone at least twelve feet wide. Having someone put it in would have cost a fortune, and they had more determination than money, so Grandma went and watched rock masons work.

When they asked her why she was there, she told them, "I want to do this at my house." They told her all the reasons she shouldn't and how many a mason does it wrong and the rock can fall. She took note of all their comments, and when she felt she had learned enough, she started scouring for rocks. She didn't order rocks, but she took her little Cub Cadet tractor/mower with a small wagon to neighbor farmer's fields and picked rocks one at a time.

When she had piles and piles of rocks, she started her rock fireplace. Grandpa made the mortar with a small cement mixer, and Grandma laid rock from bottom to top and it was beautiful!

I told Grandma that I wished I could have rock at Robert's and my house. She said to me, "You take a week off work, and Grandpa and I will come up and I will teach you how to do it. Grandpa will bring the cement mixer and make our mortar." Again, Grandma believed I could do it, so I believed I could do it, and I did.

Unlike Grandma, I didn't collect the rocks myself. Instead Robert went to Sackett Brick and ordered many tons of split field stone. Because there weren't many masons, they asked him, "Who's your mason?" He told them, "My wife and her grandma are going to do it." They looked at him like he was nuts, but a sale's a sale, so they delivered the rock on a flatbed semi-trailer to our house and unloaded the giant crates of rock around the yard.

On Memorial Day weekend, Grandma and Grandpa drove in with their motorhome and the training began. Grandpa made mortar, just as Grandma promised he would. Then, one rock at a time, Grandma, at sixty-five years old, showed me how to choose a rock that fit the space and would provide support and not fall out. She would show me how to make a strong base, using smaller stones to strengthen the mortar. She showed me how to fill in behind each stone and tamp the mortar in around it making sure there were no air bubbles which could cause the heavy rock to dislodge later. She taught me the importance of using brick ties so the wall wouldn't fall. Then, she showed me how to brace each rock until it was dry. Finally, she showed me how to use muriatic acid to clean the face of the stones when I was done.

That summer, at twenty-five years old, I took a break from college and laid rock on the whole front of my house. On average, I laid only seven rocks a day. On November 5, I placed the last rock.

There were two crates of rocks left and Robert called Sackett Brick and told them to come retrieve the extras. The man who asked Robert who his mason was, rode out with the truck driver to pick up the rock. He wanted to see this house that the grandma and her granddaughter finished. When he arrived, he said to me, "Wow! This is absolutely beautiful! Can I take your picture in front of your work?"

I was so proud of my grandma, my grandpa, and me. It was hard work. I was buff, and my house was just as I dreamed.

When we finished the house, Mr. Doster came for a visit and asked for the rest of our money. We told him that the deal was that we would buy all of materials from him and he would carry us and allow us to make payments. We'd paid a significant upcharge to him for the materials, but it was worth not having to get a mortgage. He told us he was on hard times and wouldn't be able to do it.

We were so angry! We could have saved so much money buying the materials elsewhere, but we went to the bank and got a loan to pay Mr. Doster the money we owed him. If we continued putting my whole paycheck toward the house, we figured we could probably have the house paid off in five years—by the time I was thirty!

CHAPTER 10

The Destroyer

Being in management in sales had benefits; I got to go to the national sales meetings, so I was able to travel a little. After one of the sales meetings, we all went out to dinner together. I truly enjoyed the people I worked with and found it really fun! The guys were all a lot older than me. One of the men I really enjoyed used to tell me he had socks older than me. His wife told me he loved me like his daughter and I really think he did. I adored him—he was a really big teddy bear!

After dinner, we went to a place for drinks and dancing—more fun together. A slow dance came on and one of the men, Dean, asked me to dance. He held me very close…so close that my boss was uncomfortable and actually came up to us and told him to knock it off. He didn't; he kept holding me until the song was done. I was a little uncomfortable, but it was just a dance. Afterward, we all went back to the hotel and to our rooms.

The following week when we got back to the office, Dean asked me if he could take me out and buy me a drink. I told him I didn't drink. He asked, "How about a cup of coffee?" I told him I didn't drink coffee. He asked me what I drank and I told him, "Orange juice." So he said he'd buy me an orange juice. He said he just wanted to talk to me. I told him, "Okay."

I was still going to college, so he told me where to meet him on my way home.

After class, I heard God speak to me in my head loudly for the second time. He said, "*If you go, you will never turn back.*" Unlike the first time when God told me I would be married three times, I was alarmed. And, unlike the first time, this time, I had a choice. God gave me a warning and I could heed it. I could obey.

But I didn't. I was curious, and although I was a young woman, I felt like I could hold my own against this man if things got out of hand. I was wrong.

I drove to the seedy, disgusting bar on my way home. He bought me my orange juice, and he just talked to me. I was on edge, but he was being friendly, nothing more. When I told him I had to go, he walked me to my car. He told me he wanted to see me again, and I told him, "No, I'm happily married." The fact that I wasn't was none of his business. The fact that I cried when my husband made love to me in the dark once a month was none of his business. The fact that I felt no attraction to my husband other than he was my best friend was none of his business.

I went to my car and he got in the passenger side and told me he just wanted to talk to me for a second and then he kissed me. As much as I was not interested in him, I didn't find him attractive, and he was someone I worked for, I felt something when he kissed me—a physical response to a man that I hadn't felt in ten years.

God was right. I didn't turn back.

Dean gave me romantic cards every week telling me how much he loved me. He met me on the way to work so he could kiss me. He would meet me on campus to kiss me.

I had feelings for a man who was not my husband. A man who was twenty-two years older than me. A man who was married with three boys. A man who knew better.

*****

One night when I came home from class early, I got into the house and the phone was ringing. Robert yelled out, "I'll get it," at the same time I was picking up the extension in the kitchen.

65

I heard a woman's soft voice say, "Hi, babe!" I was stunned and silent. I hung up the phone and went in the living room sitting across from Robert as he finished the conversation—cutting it short.

I asked him who she was, and he told me it was a woman he met at a teacher's conference. She lived on the other side of the state, and she was having problems in her marriage. They were just friends and nothing had happened. He told me he wouldn't talk to her any more.

If he was cheating on me, I honestly couldn't blame him. Our love life didn't exist. He was my very best friend in the world, but he was not my lover. I knew—I had one of those too.

A while later, I was sitting in the living room, and across the room in the foyer was Robert's brief case. A voice in my head said, "Open the brief case."

I never snooped through Robert's things, but the voice in my head was loud. I obeyed it. Inside his brief case was a picture of a woman and our long-distance phone bill. He was having our bill sent to his work so I couldn't see the long-distance charges to a number with an area code on the other side of the state.

When Robert came home, I asked him who it was in the picture and he told me it was the woman from the other side of the state. I left him to deal with his own guilt as I had to deal with mine.

I didn't snoop further until another while later. I again heard the voice, "Look in the brief case." I did and found long-distance calling cards. Indeed, he was having the phone bill sent to our house now, but he had found another way to communicate with this friend.

I confronted him again and he said he would cut it off. I was so hurt, but again, how could I blame him—Robert's mom told me a man had needs. She was right; a person has needs. Needs to be loved and I wasn't holding up my end of the bargain, but he had no idea how bad it actually was—he had no idea yet I was a huge cheater—a cheater that didn't just talk to someone on the phone, but it was all about to change.

*****

Dean had started to come to our house in the morning after Robert left for work. The neighbor saw him and said something to Robert. Robert was so scared and said he knew he couldn't face catching us in person, so he set up a video recorder in our house and turned it on when he left for work.

He caught us on tape. He couldn't really see anything but our feet, but he could hear enough to confirm what he really didn't want to know. I can't imagine the hurt I put him through.

When he came home, he confronted me and held up the tape. He locked me out of the house without my purse and car keys. I was stranded outside of my home with nowhere to go, so I started walking toward town. I don't know where I thought I would go, but I had to go somewhere.

The neighbor saw me walking. It wouldn't surprise me if she had heard us arguing and watched me leave. She drove after me and saw the tears running down my face. She asked me if I was okay and I told her no. She didn't say a word. She just held my hand and drove me back home. I slept in my car that night. It was cold and I was having my period, but I knew I deserved not having a bed or pillow to rest my head—I had defiled the one I had.

The next day, Robert gave me my car keys and purse and told me I needed to go stay at my parent's house—he told me I needed to tell my parents and my grandparents what I did. If I didn't, he would. He told me he didn't want his parents to know we were separated because they would never forgive me. If we wanted to get back together ever, I would need to keep it a secret, but I was no longer welcome there. He would keep all our possessions and the house so his parents wouldn't notice anything amiss. I could take my clothes and my dog.

I went to Mom and Dad's house and I cried and told them what I did.

They didn't yell; they just told me they loved me and I was welcome to stay as long as I needed.

I drove to my Grandma Van's house to tell her. Mom already called and told her in case it was too much for her to bear, but she was so gracious. Why I thought I had to marry a man I did not love because I thought my family would be disappointed if I broke up with him, I don't know. I did think those stupid things. But here in a failure bigger than breaking up with a boyfriend. My Grandma, a staunch believer in Jesus Christ, showed me grace and love in the face of my sin.

*****

Eventually I got an apartment. Robert allowed me to take my twin bed I still had from when I was little, a card table and chairs my grandparents had given us for a wedding present, and my old steamer trunk my grandpa had given me as a teen. Plus, of course, my clothes. These were things that had been in our basement, so his parents wouldn't notice they were gone. He had everything else so his parents would not be suspect that we were apart.

When I was in my apartment, I remember a visit my dad paid me that had a profound impact on me. My whole life, I made decisions about what I should do that would please others. I stayed with Robert because it would make him happy. I didn't break up with Robert because of what others would say. I was living for everyone else with no regard for my own happiness.

When Dad visited, he asked me what I wanted to do in life. What would make me happy? I didn't know. I honestly didn't know.

He told me, "I want you to think about it. And, when you know, I want you to go for it all out. No regrets. Live your life. Not for me. Not for your mother. Not for Dean or Robert. For you."

Wow. I had this choice? Of course, I did, but I didn't think about it until my dear dad gave me permission to be an adult with a mind and a vote. That day, things changed. I dared to dream about what could be for me.

In this time in 2020 when so many people are doing things for themselves with no regard for others, maybe this isn't a big deal anymore, but for me, it certainly was in the late '80s/early '90s.

God talks about being humble in heart and being a servant. He talks about how a husband should treat a wife, and how a wife should be toward her husband, but he never ever says "Women be a doormat. Give up your joy. I have no purpose for you." Far from that! There must be balance. We have permission to do what is wholesome and good. When God gives us an open door, we can go through it and walk with him. He doesn't lead us down the valley of the shadow of death. When we choose to take that path, he promises to walk with us and God did not leave me.

I have always loved the twenty-third Psalm, but as I ponder the words in my heart, they are so profound to me...

"The Lord is my shepherd, I shall not be in want. He makes me lie down in green pastures, He leads me beside quiet waters, He restores my soul. He guides me in paths of righteousness for His name's sake." He is my shepherd—He leads me, but it doesn't mean I follow. If only I had followed. If only I had obeyed, what a beautiful promise awaited me, but I did not follow Him. I did not take His path. Yet He did not abandon me. The Psalm goes on to say, "Even though I walk through the valley of the shadow of death, I will fear no evil, for You are with me; Your rod and Your staff they comfort me." Even though I walk... It was my choice not to follow my shepherd; my choice to walk through the valley. He doesn't take me there; He brings me through the valley to the other side! I am not alone. No matter where I am—no matter how far off course we go, His rod protects us from evil. He can beat Satan away and He promises to do that. When we fall from the cliff, He takes the hook of His staff and He reaches down and grabs us from around the neck and pulls us to safety *because He loves us and He died for us and we are His no matter what!*

"You prepare a table before me in the presence of my enemies. You anoint my head with oil; my cup overflows. Surely goodness and love will follow me all the days of my life, and I will dwell in the house of the Lord forever." His promise. When I am His, when you are His, His promises are there for us. No matter if we have walked through the valley or along the paths He intended for us, we are His!

Where was my church? I had stopped going to our Lutheran church.

Robert and I had been youth group leaders at one point. We stopped doing that because he was with teens all day at school and having to be with them outside of school was too much. That made me sad because we had no children of our own, which now I considered a blessing, but I loved the kids.

69

I do believe our pastor knew that we were having difficulties, but he never asked either of if we were okay. When we stopped attending, no one called. I felt abandoned.

I feel so strongly about the importance of a church family! I know people, even in my very own family, who don't feel church participation matters. I agree that God doesn't require it to be with Him in heaven, but it's a blessing *for* us and we are a blessing *to* others. Having gone through what I did alone did not help me one bit.

I didn't have a youth group to attend when I was an older teen—our church was just getting started. I went in middle school, like I shared, to the Baptist church, and their youth leaders were amazing. I wish I had a youth leader when I was I high school because I'm not so sure I wouldn't have opened up to them.

I've had the blessing, now that I'm older, of having some of the youth I mentored tell me the difference having me in their life meant to them. One guy told me just last year, he didn't know if he would still be here had I not been present in his life as a teen. He came to church twice a week when he was a teen because he was accountable to me and I was to him. We were there for each other, and he's now a youth group leader himself and he is amazing. I cry with true joy that God put us together!

I used to think prayer chains were gossip chains. Not so at the last two churches I attended. People are so open because we support each other—through divorce, sickness, death of children—maybe not always perfectly, but we are not alone.

Yes, God has spoken to me. He has shown Himself to me so many times, but He also gives us to each other. When we fall, if there are even two other arms to catch us, we won't hit the floor. Alone, falling can result in a broken hip or a broken heart or a broken family.

Find a church where there is family…where there is love, and be that love to another person who may be lost or hurt. It may seem weird or scary at first, but you don't need to say anything; just be there. God will fill in the blanks. Sometimes no words are even necessary; He gave us arms for hugging for a reason.

*****

I went to see a counselor. I was seeing him for a while and Robert gave me an ultimatum—I needed to see a counselor or he would divorce me. I told him I already was seeing someone. He went with me, but it was so hostile that the counselor told us he needed to meet with us separately.

Robert had more ultimatums. I needed to quit my job. I needed to have sex with him whenever he wanted. I was a wreck. I understood, but I didn't know if emotionally I could handle it.

When I talked to the counselor alone, he said Robert was going to attempt to leave me destitute to hurt me. If I quit my job, he felt that he would divorce me anyway, but I would be jobless. I could go through sex therapy, but he told me it would be brutal for me. He told Robert it could be years before I would be able to have normal relations with him—it took years to get to the bad place I was with him and it could take years to have it back. Robert wasn't willing to wait; he said he would file for divorce.

I'll admit I was relieved because I felt raped every time we were intimate and that was happening long before I met Dean. I knew with God's help, I was willing to try, but we were so broken!

Robert hired a different counselor to help us separate our things for the divorce. Robert met with him first and told him about my infidelity. When we met with him in our first meeting together, the counselor was extremely rude to me. Discussions quickly got hostile and the counselor told us he would talk to us separately. I told the counselor about my guilt and why I married Robert. I told him about my guilt about Dean but was relieved to know I could have feelings for someone.

The counselor apologized to me; he said he didn't realize all I had gone through and for how many years. He told me he was happy I had someone I could go to when the marriage crumbled because I wouldn't be alone. Was this biblical wisdom? No! But, I didn't care—it was an excuse to make me feel better about my extramarital relationship, even though I knew God wouldn't bless my relationship with Dean.

Robert wanted the house and I didn't care about the stuff because I was finally free of the relationship I should have ended when I was fifteen years old. I lost my very best friend, but I didn't lose my husband because he never really was my husband in my heart—and Robert got his freedom!

*****

Robert told me that I could never have contact with his family again. He told me they wouldn't forgive me and they never wanted to ever hear from me. It broke my heart in two. They had been a second family to me since I was fourteen years old—half of my life. A broken marriage isn't just losing a spouse or possessions but family. Except, he kept mine.

I rented a house from a friend for a few months. It was easy to move because I didn't have much. I was at my parents' house when Robert called one day and asked to speak to me. I answered but didn't know my dad was on the phone in another room listening. Robert told me I needed to come and get my grand piano. I explained that I had nowhere to put it and no way to move it. He told me if I didn't come and get it immediately, he would get rid of it. It was one of my only cherished possessions.

Dad's calm, deep voice said, "Diane, hang up the phone." I did.

Dad came upstairs and told me, "I always thought he was an angel, but I never heard him talk to you that way. He knows you have no place to put the one thing you love. I will get some guys to move it and I don't want you to worry about it. I never want you to have to talk to him again. If he needs anything else, he knows he is to call me."

Wow. I loved my daddy for being my daddy. For protecting me when I was alone and over my head.

*****

There was a lady that I really liked that went to our church. Her name was Joanna, and she had been married previously to some men who didn't treat her well. She was so sweet, and I didn't understand how someone could treat her badly. I prayed that God would put her and Robert together. I knew he wanted a wife who would stay at home and raise children and I thought she would be wonderful for him.

I told Mom I was praying for this. She started to cry and asked me how I could pray for my husband to marry another woman. I told her, "Mom, he is a good guy. He would make her a wonderful husband and they would be happy. I want him to be happy and I would never be that for him."

God answered my prayer, and Robert started to date Joanna and some months later they were married.

Mom and Dad proved their unconditional love to me so many times, but when I needed them most, they were rock stars. They didn't interfere but offered support when I needed them. I wish I could be a parent like them, but I will admit self-control is not my gift!

After Robert and Joanna were together, his grandmother was not doing well. Robert called my mom to tell her so she could let me know because he knew how much I loved her. I had Mom ask Robert if I could visit her to say goodbye. He said he'd think about it.

He called my mom back and told her, "No, I don't think it's a good idea. Grandma really likes Diane and she is having a hard time accepting Joanna, so I don't think she should do that." Okay, so grandma is dying...would she really ever need to accept Joanna if she was not going to live anyway? I respected his wishes and suffered another consequence of my sin. I know she's going to heaven, and I am going to love her something fierce when I see her!

When my Grandpa Koehl died a couple of years later, Robert and Joanna came to the funeral. It was okay. I didn't want to deny him saying goodbye. It's not about what's fair; it's about what's right. Being gracious is right.

A number of years later, I saw Robert's parents. I hadn't contacted them because he told me they never wanted to see me again. They were so happy to see me. I saw Mr. Smitten at a blood drive and got hugs and many smiles. I often wonder if they really said they never wanted to see me again or if Robert made it up. If he did, did they just thought I didn't care and never came to visit? Sometimes

I wish I had been braver and just continued to reach out and love them, but I was afraid and didn't want to make them uncomfortable by staying in their life.

I'll never know for sure. My dearest Mr. Smitten died a few years ago. I would drive by their house on my way home and break down crying. I missed him so terribly. I wanted to see him before he died, but what if he did say that he never wanted to see me? Dare I betray his wishes? I didn't ever stop at their house, and when he died, I broke in two.

Mom saw Mrs. Smitten after his death and she told her that their other son's ex-wife came to visit him when he was dying. Mom said I should have gone, but I know one day I will see him again and I will have eternity left with him and he can teach me to make my feet move correctly when I play the organ and how glorious it will be!

What's most important to me about Robert is that he has a wonderful life—a life full of love and joy as God intended. God absolutely replaced every possession I left behind. Happiness doesn't come from things; it's a joy from within that is nourished by those around me—whether they are human beings or God's word or the Holy Spirit. Joy comes to me when I let God take the burden—as He promises He will—in one of my most favorite verses, Matthew 11:28–30: "Come to Me all you who are weary and burdened, and I will give you rest. Take My yoke upon you and learn from Me, for I am gentle and humble in heart and you will find rest for your souls. For My yoke is easy and My burden is light."

Oh, why did I try to carry my burden alone? Why did I not give my relationship with Robert to the Lord when I was fourteen, not twenty-eight?

I only know that God knew what I would choose and He loved me anyway. He saw me through it, He refined me with fire, and I learned and I will never go there again.

Being obedient is so much easier than refining with fire! Being burned with a blow torch hurts something fierce. Why am I such a hard learner? That darn Satan knows what tempts me, and I need a closer walk with Thee! Get behind me, Satan. You're messing with a child of God!

CHAPTER 11

Hurt but Blessed

Now I was free to date Dean without hiding it. In the years I had dated him, he did end up getting divorced. He talked about us getting married.

He suggested we buy a place on a lake. I told him about Sandy Pines—a wonderful summer campground setting north of Allegan. We went to look at some places and he chose a place on a lake. He told me I should buy it. I told him I couldn't afford a lake lot—they were $30,000 and places that weren't lakefront were about $15,000.

He told me if I paid the payments in the summer when I lived there, in the winter when I had to live somewhere else (because there was a six-month residence maximum), he would pay for it.

It sounded like a great deal—being on the lake would be wonderful! So I bought the place and he came and stayed with me there. It was a wonderful summer!

Dean was planning a trip to Ireland, and he wanted me to go. Then he decided perhaps he would go alone and he did.

When he came back, he started to be more distant. By late fall, when it was time for me to move out of Sandy Pines and find a new place to live, he wasn't coming around much.

One of Mom's dearest friends, Carole Darby, had another friend who asked if I would like to talk to her. See, I now knew Mom was talking to her friends about me, but Carole is one of the strongest Christian women I have ever known, so she can know anything she wants about my personal life! Yes, of course, I would talk to Carole's friend! I didn't really want to carry my burdens alone and I indeed felt very alone!

I can't remember the lady's name, but when I told her I was so sad because I'd ruined my marriage and now was still in a relationship with this man and I didn't know if I should be… I was troubled. She told me this and I'll ever forget it:

Picture yourself as Abraham was in front of the altar when he was going to give his son Isaac to God as a sacrifice. Picture yourself laying Dean (or whatever burden) on that altar. Now, picture yourself pulling your hands away. Now watch God take Dean into his arms. There is peace in releasing our burdens to Him, but visualizing it helps. Whenever you are tempted to take the concerns about Dean back, picture God putting him back and you picking him back up. Who is better capable of caring for him?

Oh my—it was beautiful for so many reasons. When I closed my eyes and did this, the weight from my chest was gone. God was freeing me. He was taking my burden for real. When I wanted to take it all back, I pictured God placing Dean back on the altar so I could have him back. That meant I had to take Dean from God. I had to take my relationship away from God. When I asked myself, "Who should hold Dean? God or me?" I knew the answer and I could let go and let God have His way in our relationship.

When I let God take him, I started to see things that were going on much more clearly. The scales fell from my eyes.

What I didn't know was this man was not just seeing me. He was sending love cards to multiple women at the same time. I learned from a friend at work that when he traveled for business, he slept with other women. Sexual predators are real and I fell for one hard. Now, I am sickened to know that I fell for this ultimate temptation, but I realize Satan uses every tool he can and he did!

Dean finally told me that his counselor shared with him that he is a man who needs to be with many women—like this is a typical ailment that some men have like diabetes or something? So it was just a fact, I guess, and was something I could be okay with? Not!

He went on to say he never cheated on me when he loved me. He was a liar and I was a liar, and that was not okay.

I learned some things very important for myself.

- I need to finish a relationship and be healthy before moving to another one.
- Sinning with a man (or woman) never solves anything. Sin + XXXXX does not equal anything good!
- Cheating doesn't solve anything—it only makes the problems that are bad worse.
- I knew God was with me, but I was not with Him and I wasn't okay with that. It was time to start walking with God again. This life of sin was not okay.
- Satan, I am not believing your trashy lies anymore!

CHAPTER 12

Life Moves On

For a while, I moved every six months between an apartment to Sandy Pines or a house rented from a friend to Sandy Pines. I didn't have much, so all my possessions would fit in the smallest U-Haul truck available. Mom and Dad never complained about helping me because I couldn't manage lifting a small love seat by myself.

I have this appreciation for Victorian houses, and I found one in Otsego that I really liked. I called the realtor, Mrs. Mason, and told her I wanted to see the blue house on M-89 she had for sale and she said she would meet me at the house and show me through.

I went to the house and waited and waited and she never came. I called her and found she was waiting at a small blue house a few miles down the road. She asked me, "You want to see the big blue house in town? How many people do you have in your family?"

I told her, "Just my dog and me."

She laughed and set up an appointment to see the big blue house, not the little blue house.

I loved it!

Mrs. Mason was wonderful. She did all the paperwork and went with me to get a loan. I asked her if she always did this and she told me, "No, but you are very young and I am so proud of you that you are a single woman buying this big house by yourself and I don't want anyone taking advantage of you." God was sending protectors to watch over me and Mrs. Mason was a good one.

The house needed some fixing up. It was once quite a glorious home. It had gone into disrepair and was condemned. The neighbors across the street bought it and planned to tear it down, but once they started working inside, they found treasures beneath the paint that were amazing. They sold their home and worked to bring the home back to its original beauty. They'd done a good job, and it was up to me to finish what they had begun.

I was so thankful for Dad and Grandma trusting me enough to teach me how to use tools so I could work on the restorations and not have to hire it done. I think the putty knife is my favorite—I can do a lot with that tool!

The first night I moved in, Dad helped me carry my twin bed up to the big bedroom upstairs. The house was pretty empty.

The sellers had left me an amazing book telling me the history of the home. I sat down to read it and found out the man who had initially built the house had committed suicide upstairs. If I remember correctly, his wife and child died and he was so distraught, he went upstairs and killed himself. My eyes got big. Dad looked at me and asked, "Do you want to bring your bed downstairs?"

I replied, "Yes!" And so we did.

For about six months after that, I would run upstairs if I needed something and hurry back down slamming the door to the stairway behind me as I panted like the devil himself were after me.

Finally, one day, Dad said, "You know, I have senses about these things and when I come over here, I feel huge peace. Do you ever feel or hear anything?"

I told him, "No, other than my breathing when I freak out."

His peace made me relax and I moved my little bed back upstairs.

*****

As I bought things for my new, old house, I shopped for new carpet. I went to New York Carpet World and David, the "Carpet Boy," helped me find something suitable. David told me someone would come measure and install it.

When the day came for the guy to measure, David knocked on the back door. He measured everything and was very nice. I asked him, "Is it normal for the sales person to measure?"

He told me, "No, I thought you were cute."

Well, he was cute, too. He made my day.

I went out with him a couple of times and was really enjoying his company. I told Mom and Dad about him, and they wanted to meet him. Dad said, "Call me when he comes over. See if you can get him down on the floor after you see me drive past the window when I come into the driveway. Make sure the back door is unlocked so I can get in the house."

I didn't want to know what he had up his sleeve, but I knew it would be fun and I'm all about fun. So, the next time David came over, I let Dad know. About ten minutes later, I saw Dad's car go past my window.

I told David, "You know, there is some crunching noise under the carpet and I don't know what it is, but something's not right."

Pleased to help me in any way he could, and because he had a responsibility to take care of his carpet customer, he got on his hands and knees and started pushing on the carpet trying to hear the noise. Nothing. I told him maybe it was a little further over here. David kept trying to push down and hear the noise.

Soon, Dad entered the room wearing a trench coat, a big floppy hat, and a muzzle loader slung over his arm. He yelled, "Boy, what are you doing on my daughter's floor?"

David's eyes got huge. He jumped up and backed up until he hit the wall screaming, "Nothing, sir! I'm just checking the carpet!" His face was red, and I thought he was going to pass out.

That's when Dad started laughing. He reached out his hand and said, "Hi, I'm Ted; Diane's dad. Nice to meet you."

David laughed hesitantly and took his hand. I don't think he got closer than a couple of feet from him for a while. He seemed a little more comfortable meeting Mom.

I thought it was wonderful! I was having fun!

David wasn't a believer, but I shared with him what God had done in giving me my dad back and seeing me through my life. David listened. Seeds were planted for sure.

Mom loved David and I did too, but I couldn't see me marrying him and I was not going to make the mistake again of marrying someone because I couldn't break it off. So I told him. It made us both sad, but I truly cared about his happiness and I needed to set him free. I think he really loved me and I loved him too, but not as a potential husband.

I saw David many years later. He had gone from selling carpet to cars. When I pulled in, I'd just gotten a perm or something and didn't want him to see me. I pulled the visor down and drove away. I went back later after I was put together and he told me, "I saw you the other day and you drove off. What happened?" I had to confess... because David is the type of guy that is so dear, I had to tell him.

He was so excited to see me! He told me that he was a believer. He shared with me that he had been baptized in his friend's shower after he accepted Christ and he bawled like a baby. I was smiling so big for him. He was so happy!

He went on to tell me that his grandfather had died and he was in the room at the time. He said, "Diane, I need to tell you something because I know you will understand. Diane, when my grandpa died, I saw an angel come to get him. Diane, it was amazing! I saw him! And, when grandpa stopped breathing, the angel was gone. Do you believe me?"

I told him I truly did and what a miracle that he was able to see this. I told him I do not believe we are alone when we die and he was able to see that this was true. He saw the angel that brought his grandpa home. What a gift that I got to see my friend again and he blessed me with his faith story.

Such joy. Thank you, God, for placing people in my life and for letting me live long enough to see those threads that you wove through my journeys turning into a beautiful tapestry. Thank you, God, for letting me see planted seeds grow to harvest. David was God's blessing to me.

*****

I am not a woman who likes to shop. I've been told I don't go shopping, I go buying. That's probably true. I enjoy a list that is put together in the order of the store and now I know there are apps for that.

One of the other things I needed for my home besides carpet was an answering machine. I had to go to a different store for that, so I did.

There another nice young man helped me out making sure I would select one that suited my needs (of course, it had to be cheap).

I got home and hooked it up—I figured it out and was pretty proud of myself. Once again, I was finding that I could take care of myself being alone for the first time in my life.

The phone rang, and surprise, it was Ron—the salesman from the store, calling to make sure I was able to hook up my answering machine properly. Seriously?

I asked him, "Do you always call to make sure the customers are happy with their purchase?

He said, "No, I thought you were cute. Can I ask you out?"

Oh my goodness! I never knew I was cute. Maybe Heidi wasn't the only one who was going to have a paper chain with a boy's name on every link!

I didn't date Ron for too long. He was a lot younger than me. (I mean he was legal and I was in my late twenties, but I think eight years at that age is too much!) Besides Ron's mom looked at me with concern when I helped him deliver a beautiful rhododendron to her for Mother's Day. It's like she could sniff out a cougar or something.

I didn't do any shopping after that for a while—the side effects were too time-consuming.

CHAPTER 13

God Calls Dad

Ever since Dad had been a believer, his faith had continued to grow. He and Mom did marriage enrichment classes, and he actually filled in as a lay preacher when their pastor was out of town.

People told Dad he had a gift and he should become a preacher. It was nice affirmation for him, I'm sure. Dad said the day that the bishop told him he should become a pastor, he would consider it.

Of course, you can guess what happened. Our pastor told Dad he should talk to the bishop and made an appointment for Dad to go to the Synod office in Lansing. The bishop told Dad he should go to seminary.

On the way home, Dad saw a bumper sticker that said, "I said it, you did it and that's that!" Yeah, like this happens all this time. Dad came home and told Mom he thought he should go into the ministry.

Mom and Dad called a realtor. If he was going to seminary, they would have to move to Ohio, which meant selling the house Dad built. Plus, college wasn't free. He had done some checking and the seminary would allow him to skip finishing his bachelor's and get his masters of divinity. He'd had a lot of schooling and it didn't make sense for him to finish general ed classes because he was forty-eight years old. College would cost him $72,000.

The realtor came. Thankfully Mom and Dad had enough money to finish the house over the years and despite the treachery of the driveway, they got an offer on the house within a week. Once they sold it and took out what they owed, she said they'd clear $72,000.

The answer was clear and a little too large to ignore. Mom and Dad were moving to Ohio.

We started the move. They packed the belongings they wouldn't be able to put in their apartment in my carriage house. Dave, a friend from work who was recently single and a really nice guy, asked if he could help them move because he had nothing to do.

Dave found out his wife of only one year had a boyfriend. He was devastated—he was still in the honeymoon stage of his marriage. I offered to let him stay on the main floor of my house because I was at Sandy Pines for the summer. Billy and his wife, Sue, were living upstairs, but the house was big and they worked second shift, so they wouldn't see each other much. Dave liked my brother a lot, so he kind of became part of the family.

Mom and Dad, Dave, and Grandma June all helped with the caravan to their new apartment. It was really weird being a kid and having my parents move out and go away to school. But it was also amazing to know that my dad was following the Lord's calling— especially knowing where he came from.

Dad said one thing was for sure, he'd never judge anyone because he knew he had no place to do that. He'd been one of the worst, and if God could forgive him, who was he to judge? Amen!

The night we arrived in Ohio, we got a lot unpacked, and Mom made Dave and me a little bed on the floor. Dave and I didn't have a clue what to do or say. My mom made a bed for me and a guy on her living room floor? A preacher's wife-to-be made one bed for us? Dave and I did not sleep together! He was my friend! Since neither of us knew what to do, we climbed under the covers and faced away from each other all night. Later, I told Mom and she was horrified! "I made my daughter sleep with a man!" Haaa! It actually was quite hysterical—afterward, Dave and I could laugh about it.

*****

I was now managing the art department, which was a huge promotion for me. I was making $28,000 per year (which is ridiculously not much, but when I started at $12,500, I felt very rich). I loved the job and the people I worked with. I was super excited to be invited to a Halloween party at the home of one of my employees even though it was really last-minute.

I had no idea what to wear, but leave it to my sister-in-law, she fixed me right up. In her strong New York accent, she said, "I know! You're gonna be a hoo-er." I looked at her confused and asked, "What's a hoo-er?" My brother answered, "A whore!"

"What?" I said. "I can't go as a whore!"

She said, "Yes, you can, Daa-link! I have all of the clothes. I can do you up."

Now I began to question exactly how my brother met his wife when he was in New York. The story was they met when they were both working at a country club, but was there more?

She put me in a short spandex black dress that just covered my bum. Sue said I had to wear it backward. It had a plunging back and she made me wear a bright pink tube top underneath. Then, she gave me fishnet stockings and immensely high stilettos. Over all of this, I wore a fur coat the same length as the dress. She ratted my hair, gave me earrings, huge sunglasses, and a cigarette. When she was done creating her masterpiece from hell, my sister arrived with her husband and my niece and nephew for trick-or-treating. Not great! My innocent niece and nephew got to see their naughty aunt!

My brother-in-law wasn't too partial to me. I didn't really appreciate the way he treated my sister, but he took one look at me, wiped the drool from his chin, and asked, "Can Heidi borrow that outfit when you're done?"

Heidi smacked him and said, "No!"

With no further "improvements" to make, I headed to Harding's Friendly Market to pick up a beverage for the party. I definitely needed to BYOB since I didn't drink much besides orange juice. When I was in the refrigerated section, a little old man looked up to see me and immediately shielded his eyes to stare at the floor. I had forgotten that I looked like this, but if he went to Robert's parent's church, the old man was headed for the confessional soon.

I got to the check out and the lady said, "Oh my gosh! You look real!" I told her, "Yeah, there is a guy back there that you may want to check on soon—I think he may have had a heart attack."

I had to stop and get gas before driving an hour to the party. I learned my lesson—I wasn't going to be seen again in public, so I pulled into the one full-service station left in town. The guy took one look at me and washed my front window, my side windows, my side view mirrors... I had to tell him when the pump shut off because he was still cleaning the window beside my face. Well, I don't know that he saw my face—he was cleaning the window beside my cleavage.

I finally got to the party, and one of the guys from work opened the door. He looked at me and just said, "Hi," and he didn't move. The guy throwing the party said, "Jim, why do you have the door open?" and he came to see. He looked at me and just stared. For crying out loud, it was freezing, and I was standing there with not much on other than fishnet stockings when finally the blood went back to their brains and they let me in.

It was terrible. No other girl or wife there would speak to me. I sat alone on the sofa. The guys couldn't talk to me either or their wives would have surely made them sleep in their cars in the cold without their purse or car keys.

Steve, who hosted the party, later showed me he had taken pictures of all the guests, including me, and told me he could use them against me if he ever needed to do that. He thought it was truly hysterical to have hoo-er pictures of his boss.

Heidi sent Dad a copy of the pictures she took of me and my garb. He loved it. He proudly put it in a frame and set it in his study carrel at seminary. In the frame on the left was a picture of me doing my Bible Study Fellowship homework (me by day) and on the right was a picture of the hoo-er (me by night). He said he had a lot of guys that wanted to know if they could date his daughter.

"Daaad! That's not funny!"

"Oh yes, it is!" (He is a crazy and funny preacher man!)

*****

When Dad did his internship in West Virginia, the congregants had to rate him. They gave him exceptional ratings.

When people graduate, they are appointed to their first church. The guy from Virginia said he'd give up all his choices for candidates if he could have Dad. That was quite a compliment. God had given Dad a gift for preaching!

Dad graduated from seminary and took a position as a pastor in Fishersville, Virginia. It was a church that was dying, and Dad didn't mind being so far from home because they only had enough money to pay him for two years. Then, he'd be released and he could come home to Michigan and pick his next church.

They loved it there, and we loved him being there. The church grew. In two years, they hadn't dipped into their money at all. Dad stayed six years, and the church is still in existence. I'm proud of him!

From there, he was called to a church in the Upper Peninsula. I didn't want them to live there—it was sixty degrees when we packed their belongings in Virginia and they had snow up to the roof in Chassell.

Mom said, "You know what happened to Jonah when he said he wouldn't go!

I asked her, "Do you think they have whales in Lake Superior?"

She said, "Maybe, but I don't want to find out!"

Mom said she prayed that God would change her heart about going because she didn't want to leave her friends and the beauty of Virginia. God answered her prayers. They had a wonderful life in the UP, and when Dad finally retired, they did move back to Southwest Michigan.

Living far away from us all that time wasn't what we'd wish for, but they were doing God's work and it was so wonderful! He doesn't make mistakes. We don't always wish for what we get, but there is a purpose. My Dad was a blessing and he planted and harvested many seeds.

Dad has Alzheimer's now. His goal was to live past seventy-two because none of the men in his family did that. He's seventy-six and he was diagnosed a number of years ago. Dad's doctor says he's a miracle because his disease is progressing so incredibly slowly. He still fills in and preaches sometimes and he can still give a good sermon—it's just now he has to write it down so he doesn't forget the message God gives him before he preaches it.

I'm sad that his mind, the thing God used to do his work, is being taken from him, but Dad is so good about it! He takes it one day at a time and treasures the days he is given. When he feels foggy, he goes for a bike ride or walk and the increased circulation lifts his fog.

Doctors say the fact that he does this and exercises his mind to preach is probably a lot of what helps. God knows. I think God isn't done with him yet, and when He is, my dad will certainly hear, "Well done, My good and faithful servant."

The Bible is full of stories of God using the sinner to bring people to Him. It almost seems the more remarkable the conversion to Christianity, the more powerful the draw the Holy Spirit has on our heart. When I think of Dad, I see that. People love him. God brought him from the depths and used him to draw people to our Lord.

There is nothing God won't forgive. No sin too great to prevent us from entering into His kingdom and living with God forever. I'm so thankful for God's grace. He is sooo good!

How God decides which family we will be born into is beyond my understanding, but I am thankful that He put me here. I am so ever thankful! Give thanks to God in all things!

CHAPTER 14

Husband #2

I love VW bugs!—old ones that have a motor that purrs. The engine noise from one is amazing; there's nothing like them.

I found one, but it needed a little work. A lady who worked for me said one of the guys that worked for her husband in the lawn care business was a real motorhead, and he could fix anything. She said she could have him give me a call.

He did. His name was Stony Greyson, and he said he'd stop by. I was not prepared for the hulk of testosterone that showed up in my driveway.

Please understand, I had dated nice boys, business people, and clean-looking men—not bad boys. I was totally unprepared for how to handle a man with a hairy chest and biceps. Not good!

He told me he was living with a girl. They had dated, but they didn't anymore. She had moved here from North Carolina with him. He had come back to Michigan to get away from the drugs. The girl he lived with had a job in accounting where I worked and she was looking for another place to live. He had been in prison for shooting a police officer at one point in his life, thus the prison tattoo. He had partied with Don Johnson, but he was clean now.

Um—okay; never met a guy with a rap sheet. But here's where my naïveté came into play. My past was my past, not my present. I shouldn't judge because I wouldn't want someone to do that to me. He deserved a clean present just like I did. I fell for it and him.

He fixed my car. I should have paid him and said thank you, but he was smooth.

I couldn't go to his apartment because he didn't like to rub other women in his friend's face. Um, now I know he was cheating on her, but I was such an idiot—I believed him and wouldn't want to hurt her. *Sooo stupid.* (Sorry, Grandma Van, there's that word again!)

Eventually she found out about us and broke up with him and moved back to North Carolina. That poor girl, but I know it was the right thing for her because I won the booby prize.

He went to church with me. His family loved me. They later told me they thought he was changed because he was going to church and they'd never seen him like this. They didn't dare say anything because they didn't want me to leave because with me, he was so much better (than the druggie, womanizing hoodlum he was?).

*****

Because he was a lawnmower guy with no money, I paid for my wedding ring. Yes, you read that right—wedding ring.

The proposal was romantic though. He was mowing my lawn at Sandy Pines and came inside and said, "Here, I can't mow with this thing in my pocket. Will you marry me?" Every girl's dream proposal! I said yes. I should have been exterminated—no, he should have been exterminated.

A few weeks before our wedding, he got mad. I don't remember what the argument was about. He had a temper and I was scared, really scared! I fled the house and got into my car. I didn't have the car keys, but at least I was out of the house. I hit the lock button knowing he couldn't get to me. He stood there screaming at me and then my security blanket ripped wide open as he kicked the window out beside my head sending small shards of glass shattering all over me.

I think the realization about what he did flipped his switch to off and he left.

He later returned. He was all calm and sorry.

I told him I wouldn't marry him unless we saw a counselor.

One would think that after marrying one guy because I was worried about what people would say, when the next suitor kicked a window out on top of me, I'd say, "Outta here!" but what was I going to tell the people that were invited to the wedding? I was going to my Lutheran church again and they had decorated the Christmas tree in our wedding colors—they were so excited for me! I didn't want to embarrass myself—Mr. Counselor, please tell me it's okay.

And he did. The counselor said since I had never witnessed this type of behavior before, it was probably nerves about getting married that set him off and I shouldn't call off the wedding. It would be fine.

Yes, I often hear that people that are nervous about getting married kick windows out onto their fiancée while they cower in a locked car! *Sarcasm!* But I was so relieved to have validity to not call it off and risk embarrassing myself. I dismissed all the sirens going off in my head and plowed forward.

Do you think I asked God even once about this? No, I did not! I was living life on my own again. I was worrying about what others thought instead of what God was telling me.

Satan knew what temptations would work on me—a hunky guy—and I fell for it.

On December 31, 1994, I married husband #2.

I wore the most pretty pink pearl dress. Dad couldn't believe I wanted a pink dress, but when he saw it, he said it was really, really beautiful. He was thinking Pepto Bismol, and it wasn't that at all. It had buttons all the way down the back and the train was long. I still have it on a mannequin, and I would love for someone to wear it again. It was lovely. I got it on sale for $250 because it was last year's model. (How do wedding dresses have a model year?)

I made all the food for the reception myself. We got married at Hope Lutheran and had the reception there, too.

Carole Darby had to shoo me out of the kitchen fifteen minutes before the wedding telling me to go get dressed. I told her I needed to take the last of the things out of the oven. She firmly but politely informed me that she knew how to take rolls out of the oven! I love her!

I got ready in fifteen minutes and became Mrs. Stony Greyson.

*****

I had never tried to get pregnant. I had been on the pill since I married Robert. For all I knew, I was sterile. People told me it can take a long time to get pregnant after you go off it.

One month later, I didn't feel very good. I told Mom how I felt and asked her if I could be pregnant. She said, "No, it doesn't feel like the flu when you are pregnant." After two weeks of feeling sick, I went to the doctor.

The nurse asked me if I could be pregnant and I told her, "My mom said no."

She asked, "But could you be?"

I replied, "Well, yeah, I guess so."

She came back in the room after a few minutes and said, "I'm not supposed to tell you this. It's the doctor's job, but your mom doesn't know everything."

Oh my—I was pregnant!

I went home and crawled into bed. I definitely did not feel glowing.

When Stony came home from work, he asked me what the doctor said. I told him, "I'm pregnant." He couldn't believe it, but he was so excited! He called everyone. I didn't even get to tell one person. But I couldn't really be mad at him. He was over the moon.

I think being pregnant was horrible. I spent three months hanging on to the bar in the handicap bathroom at work wishing I could die. Then I was fine for a bit and then I turned into a huge woman with feet three times their normal size.

My dear friend, Martin, from work told me I could get new clothes from Kalamazoo Tent and Awning. Heidi was so tiny when she had her kids. I guess we're different in every other way, so why should this surprise me. People said Martin was terrible for saying that, but I thought he was hysterical. I was sooo tiny before getting pregnant that it was largely incredible I could get so big.

I didn't want to know what I was having—I think peeking at Christmas presents is possibly an unforgiveable sin and peeking into my womb was similar. Actually, I just really love surprises.

We had gone through birthing classes, and I didn't care how badly it hurt. I was thirty-one and I didn't know if I'd ever have a child, so I wanted to experience it all. They told me the percentage of women who had C-sections and it meant that one of us in the class would have one, but it wasn't going to be me!

Stony was super excited about being a dad. None of the warnings that I had before the wedding showed themselves. He was in church with me all the time. It was good. It was very good.

*****

For Christmas, I loved buying presents for families in need that I didn't know. I get very little joy about getting a present. My friend Tim told me I needed to not be that way because I deprive people that love me if I don't learn to receive. He's right. I am bad that way and I do need to be more considerate about that, but if I could, I would wish for God to make me a Santa.

Finding a family to bless at Christmas was sometimes a challenge, but I found that when I called the school, even though there are privacy rules, they were willing to find a family with need that had fallen through the cracks.

The school put me in touch with a dad who worked, but his salary just didn't stretch far enough. The dad called me and I told him I wanted to buy some special things for the kids and for him and his wife. He was so touched.

He told me what the kids wanted but told me he and his wife would just appreciate us taking care of the children. He had one favor. He didn't want the kids to be home when we delivered the gifts. I think he really wanted us to be Santa. I loved it. We set a time to come, and he would have the kids at their grandparents' house.

When we got there with the presents for the kids and lots of food for mom and dad, we helped carry the stuff inside and noticed that they had no heat—they were warming the house by leaving the kitchen's electric stove door open.

He seemed a little embarrassed and told us that their fuel oil had run out, but they owed from the previous delivery and until they paid that, they couldn't get more. We said we understood and wished them a Merry Christmas. He was so happy about the gifts.

It was Christmas Eve. When we left, I started crying and I told Stony, "We are not going home. We are going to get them fuel oil, and I am going to pay that bill and get them a full tank. I don't care if we have no gifts this year—that family has no heat for their home and it's frigid outside!"

Stony knew better than to argue when I'm like this, so we headed to the fuel oil company that was only a few miles away. Miraculously, they were working, but they were about done and wouldn't be back until after the weekend because it was a holiday. I told them, "I need to have some fuel oil now. There is a family without heat." I looked in the back of Stony's truck, and there were gas cans. I asked him, "Why can't we use those?" He said, "It will ruin them." I just kept staring at him. He told the guys, "Fill them up please."

I was so happy! We headed back to their house. We didn't knock. Stony backed his truck up to the tank, climbed up, opened the top, and poured the fuel in.

The man came out with tears in his eyes and said "Thank you! Thank you so much!" Stony looked so pleased—he had done something good for someone else. I loved him extra hard for it.

Stony told him, "On Monday, they are going to fill your tank. It's a gift from us."

Then we looked in the doorway, and two little faces peered out. One of them asked in their sweet little voice, "Is that them? Are those the people who brought the presents?"

Their dad smiled and said, "Yes, they are."

My biggest present that year was seeing those tiny faces and knowing that night, they slept in a warm bed.

For years and years, when I act in love, God always picks up the tab. Somehow, extra money comes in that I didn't plan. I truly believe He refills our cups and they will never run dry if we have faith like the widow in 1 Kings 17:8–24. Elijah asks the widow for a cake of bread. She had only enough flour and oil to make a little meal for her and her son and then they would die. But he tells her to bring it anyway and she does. Because she trusted, she had food every day for Elijah, her son, and herself.

God really does work this way when we are a vessel that we let Him use. He'll give us what we need in the vessel, and we just need to pour it out when He tells us. It won't run out—I should say, it hasn't run out yet and I love watching what He does. I praise you, Lord, for letting me be a witness to the ever-filling miracle—whether it be fuel oil or a little loaf of bread! Thank You, God, for Your providence!

If you haven't trusted Him in making faith steps like this, I encourage you to step out. *He is amazing!* Giving in secret ways like this has truly been a blessing to me that has changed who I am and strengthened my faith so much. He is real, no doubt, for in this way, I have seen God provide in ways that no human could explain!

*****

One day at work, my water started leaking. I made the mistake of telling my secretary who called Stony. She told me I needed to go to the hospital. I told her, "I need to finish just one more memo!" That probably resulted in her making the phone call to Stony. The next thing I knew, Stony was pounding on my office window telling me it was time to leave. They were so pushy, but I just need to finish things!

We got to the hospital and they told me the baby was breech. They tried to turn the baby, but it wasn't changing position, so I was going to have a Cesarean. I was disappointed a little. Dr. Savage asked me if I was feeling any discomfort. I told him I wasn't. He was shocked; he said I was having really hard contractions. I told him I was feeling some pressure. I know I have a really high pain tolerance—yep—that confirmed it. Darn it, I think I would have liked to deliver naturally!

After they draped me in surgery, I asked if I could watch. The surgeon looked at me and asked, "Really? You want to watch me cut you open?"

I did, but she wouldn't take down the sterile field and there were no mirrors that would allow me to watch. Plus, she said it would make her nervous. She told Stony he could video tape it if he stood back. He was so freaked out and didn't want to watch—he couldn't figure out how to work the video camera. He took pictures for me with the regular camera, but they were lost/stolen when I sent them to be developed. I guess I wasn't meant to watch, and that bums me out to this day!

When the baby came out, it was a girl. Stony was over the moon. He wanted a girl so much! I just wanted a healthy baby, but I did want a girl. I told myself it was a boy so I wouldn't be disappointed. We weren't disappointed at all!

Heidi and her kids came right away, and they got to hold little Abigail Lee Greyson before I did. She was cute from the first second!

I had arranged for daycare so I could go back to work. Stony's parents told me they were too old to watch the baby. I reassured them that I would never expect them to watch her. But, when they held her for the first time, Thelma told me, "This baby ain't going to no daycare. I'm going to take care of her."

She was a good little baby, and when it was time for me to go back to work, she went to Mawmaw and Pawpaw's house. She was everything to them. God's plan for this was perfect because they didn't live long after Abbie started school, but she remembers them because she spent so much time with them. They used to tell me I could just leave her there during the week and come get her on the weekend. Not! She was sooo loved!

*****

Things were wonderful until Abbie was six months old. Then the scary Stony came back. I don't know what flipped his switch. Drugs? Other women? Me being twenty-five pounds heavier than I was before I got pregnant? I'm not sure, except life got scary at home.

I think a big part of our issue was that I wouldn't let him push me around. When he told me to do something that wasn't okay, I wouldn't and I don't think he liked that at all. I had learned one thing from my first relationship; I wasn't going to be a doormat.

I went on a business trip with another lady from work. When I left, I took extra credit cards out of my purse. I didn't want to lose them. I also left my checkbook; I wouldn't need that on my business trip. As I laid them on top of the dryer, I had a bad feeling that I shouldn't leave them out, but who was going to take them? Listen to the little voice.

When I came back, I got the weirdest call from my bank. Stony had come in to withdraw all the money from my account. The lady felt something wasn't right. She took a copy of his driver's license. I thanked her profusely.

Then I called the credit card companies. He had used them. On one, he bought a new expensive lawnmower for $6,500 on a card with my name only. I found out the store where he made the purchase and called them. They were freaked out. I was furious. I asked them if he looked like a Diane because that's the name he signed on the card. They got very nervous and told me no and said they'd make it right. They contacted him right away. They did and they took the charge off my card.

He had taken a cash advance on the other card up to the maximum allowed based on my credit.

When I confronted him, I told him that the money he took from the checking account wasn't mine—it was an expense check from work and I had to use it to pay bills. I told him he stole from my work!

He was caught and furious. He shoved me up against the door with his hand around my throat. I was so scared! He finally let me go and left.

I called an attorney and asked what to do. I was scared to death that he would take everything, and, unlike Robert, he had earned none of it and I was definitely a bear protecting my lair.

The attorney told me to file for divorce. He said I didn't need to go through with it, but it would prevent him from legally taking anything more. I did.

I went to Sandy Pines and I found a tampon on the trash and a Mickey Mouse watch next to my bed. Neither were mine. I called Stony and he told me he had let a friend stay there with his kids while I was gone to California and they were probably theirs. I knew he was lying to me. He had been there with someone else.

Abbie and I spent time at Sandy Pines. One time we were there alone and the tornado warnings went off. The biggest fear I have about trailer parks is tornados. It was early in the morning, and we were still in our pajamas. I grabbed Abbie, threw on my flip-flops, and headed to the car to drive to the shelter. When I hit the wooden steps going down from my trailer, my flip-flops slid on the wet steps and my feet came out from under me. I held on to Abbie tightly even when my back struck the edge of the steps. I managed to pick myself up with her still in my arms and made it to the car only to find that I had left the golf cart parked behind my vehicle. We had no choice but to take the golf cart to shelter. Through the driving rain and in excruciating pain, I floored the accelerator. The lurching cart further heightened my back pain, but I clutched Abbie and drove as fast as my little golf cart would go.

When we got there, people helped us scurry inside. The pain was searing through me, and I thought I'd pass out. I sat her on the top of a washer. She was safe, and that's what I cared about most.

Finally, someone looked at me and asked me if I was okay. They told me I didn't look so good. I wasn't. I was sweating so profusely from the pain that I stunk. I've never had that type of pain before. I told the people what had happened. They were really concerned for me, but there was really nothing they could do.

Eventually the sirens stopped and they helped me carry Abbie back to the golf cart, and I carefully drove home. Still in our PJs, I got my purse, put her in her car seat, and drove myself to the hospital. On the way to the hospital, I passed Stony in his truck with a woman sitting beside him in the middle of the front seat. My husband was with another woman when his wife and child were in danger. God help me!

At the hospital, they confirmed I had a compression fracture. There was nothing they could do but get a prescription for pain killers. Still in my pajamas, I drove to the pharmacy. I was wet and a mess, but I didn't care who saw me. I just wanted to get home.

I took Abbie to her Mawmaw's house. I told her what happened. She gave me some dry clothes and offered to watch her until I could get cleaned up and my pain was under control. I felt so badly for her.

It was then that she finally told me that they had hoped Stony had changed, but this is the type of thing he did. He'd been through lots of women, and he didn't know how to treat someone. She was so sorry. I can't imagine her sorrow or her shame. She was so good to me!

I was in Bible Study Fellowship at the time, and it was so hard because I had women tell me that if I believed God would change him, He would. They said I shouldn't get divorced because divorce was wrong and I wasn't trusting God. I heard them, but I also knew that they weren't living through what I was—I was afraid—physically afraid!

My poor parents were in Virginia. Dad recently had someone in his congregation shoot his wife. The pain of being that far away and knowing he couldn't help me had to be so hard. He sent me a book to read that gave me hope. The book talked about a man's responsibility to treat his wife with love. Abuse is not approved by God. He told me that God can change him. Maybe he would be my husband #2 and #3, but not if I was dead. He told me the Bible is clear about how a husband is to treat a wife and this was not what Stony was doing. He was so supportive of me getting away—of being safe and letting God take him.

Thank you, Dad, for speaking the truth and for giving me permission to set aside the guilt and be safe. Nothing is too big for God. God will protect me. He will see me through the valley of the shadow of death and He was about to do it again.

*****

In the depths of despair, I remember how I felt when I was alone in this grief. I sat in my living room and sobbed out to God.

The tears were dripping from my chin. I was crying so much that I could barely breathe—my body racking in grief. God, oh God, I need you to hold me—I shouted to Him! God, I need a hug! I don't want to ask a woman to hold me because that's not the hug I need. I don't need a wimpy girl-armed hug, I need a hug that's big and strong and my dad is in Virginia, but, God, it's what I need *sooooo* badly!

In my pain and sorrow, God answered my prayer. Beyond my dreams, I didn't expect what happened. He answered my prayer bigger than I could think possible. I saw God sitting large before me. His lap was huge. I felt Him reach down and pick me up and put His arms around me in the most encompassing hug. I can explain what it was like because when I was a very small child, I was held like this—fully enveloped. How many years had it been since I was that small, but within the Father's arms, I was that small because He was big.

He held me. He held me like when I was a child. He held me until the sobbing stopped. He held me until I was calm. He gave me the peace that surpasses all understanding.

I was going to be okay. Nothing is impossible with God. Nothing. Absolutely nothing. If He wants to show up in your living room and hold you, He can and He did that for me.

*****

Stony wanted to take Abbie and me to the Toledo Zoo for my thirty-fifth birthday. I told myself it would be okay. He borrowed his parents' big Chevy van with the nice cushy seats, and he drove us there.

We had a nice day at the zoo—she and I both love animals.

On the way back, she was tired. She was crying. She was two, but Mawmaw spoiled her rotten and she still had a bottle. Now they have great sippy cups, but this was over twenty years ago. Stony was getting upset because she wouldn't quit crying. He was yelling at me to fill her bottle faster so she would be quiet.

I told him I was going as fast as I could. I was trying. I was so scared—he was so angry and it was over such a small thing.

He pulled the van over to the side of the road. I slid the passenger side door back and jumped out of the van; I just wanted to get away from his degrading, life-sucking comments. He jumped out and came running after me. Once he reached me, he dragged me by the hair pulling my body backward through the crushed stone on the side of the road. I was crying and screaming for him to stop. Then he pushed me back in the van and sped off.

A trucker traveling on I-80/90 saw what happened. He didn't just ignore what he witnessed; he called the police.

When I got back in the van and Stony started to drive toward home again, he looked at Abbie and he told her he was sorry. He asked her if she was mad at Daddy and she said, "Yes."

Dear God, what my child just saw and heard, no child should ever witness.

That trucker followed our van, and when the Ohio State Police pulled us over, he pulled over too.

One officer talked to Stony and asked him to get out of the van.

Another officer came along the side and looked at me and asked me if I was okay.

I answered a meek "Yes."

He was the biggest man I'd ever seen and he was here to rescue me.

He kindly asked me, "If you're okay, then what is this?" and he pulled a large clump of hair that was hanging loosely from the side of my head.

I started to cry.

He told me I was going to be okay.

Stony was calling to me. I'm assuming he was handcuffed against the police car behind me, but I couldn't see him. He was calling me horrible names screaming profanities at me. A few minutes later, he was calling to me telling me he loved me.

The officer asked to see the rocks imbedded in my butt cheeks—apologizing to me for putting me through it. He asked me what happened and I explained. He took pictures.

Then he looked at me and he said, "You need to take your baby and you need to go home. He is nuts. He will kill you. I want you to promise me you'll never go back."

I nodded my head and told him, "Okay."

I was done. This big wonderful man was speaking the truth to me.

Then he asked me if he could give Abbie a stuffed animal. He wanted to do something nice for us. She was so happy when he gave it to her.

I got in the driver's seat, put the van into drive, and I never looked back.

I was definitely shaken up. A few hours down the road, I pulled over to a hotel and got a room. I called Mawmaw and Pawpaw and told them we were okay and we would be home the next day. I didn't go into details.

We slept until about seven thirty in the morning when there was a knock at the door. It was Stony's parents. After I called them, they left home. They had stopped at every hotel on I-80/90 until they found us. They told me we were going to go pick Stony up from jail—all the way back in Ohio past where I had started.

I was stunned and didn't know what to say! I didn't know what to do. I felt like I was held hostage in their van. Stony's dad kept telling me, "He really is a good boy. Everything's going to be just fine." Dear God, he is not a nice boy. He is an awful man!

I remember that we went to get him and I don't remember much else about the trip home, but I do know that when I got home, our marriage was over for sure.

After we got home, Stony called me and he wanted me to pay his friend Jaime $2,000. He claimed that she had given him the money to get out of jail because he couldn't get a hold of me. I told him I wouldn't pay it.

Six months or so later, I got a call from the Ohio State Police. They wanted to know if I wanted the evidence to press charges. I told them no. I just wanted to never relive any of this. He gave me his phone number in case I changed my mind. I think they had my hair and pictures of my butt cheeks and I really didn't care to see any of that.

After I hung up, I called him back. I wasn't sure how deep Stony's lies went, but I doubted that Jaime ever gave him money, but I hoped they could tell me.

I asked them where the money came from to post Stony's bail. He hesitated and sounded confused. He said there was no money required to get him out of jail. They just kept him overnight and then he was free to go. I had the information I needed. Stony had used his night in jail as an excuse to give him money for his girlfriend.

*****

One of the passions Stony and I shared in our marriage was a love for classic cars. In the few years we were married, I had owned an older Porsche 911, a couple of Ford Mustangs, and a VW Bug convertible. It was the nice thing about having a motorhead for a husband! My VW Bug and my mustang were in storage in Stony's parents' pole barn. I had driven the bug only once since having it shipped from California to Michigan and was really looking forward to spring!

I was sitting on my front porch, and I saw a white convertible VW bug go by. I knew that sound, so when I heard it, I looked up and thought, "That looks like my car!" Oh my gosh—what if Stony sold it and stole the money. But I had the titles in my possession, so it couldn't be mine, but the nagging feeling wouldn't leave!

I called the secretary of state and found out, yes, the VW bug was no longer in my name. I told them what happened and they sent me a copy of the title. Stony filled out a lost and stolen title form and had signed my name—in his handwriting. He had done exactly what I feared. When I asked about the Mustang, they told me it was still in my name, but it was only because the title transfer hadn't cleared. A week later, I found out both cars were gone.

When I talked to my lawyer about it, I said it was grand theft auto. He told me that I would never be able to prove that I didn't allow him to sell the cars; husbands and wives sign each other's names all of the time. He did tell Stony's attorney that he would get nothing from me in the divorce because he had stolen enough, and if he didn't agree, we would press charges about the cars. He agreed.

God, how low can someone go?—lower than I ever wish to be!

Because I didn't want to file taxes jointly with someone I couldn't trust, I asked if there was any way that my divorce could be final before the end of the year. My wonderful attorney talked to the judge and he came in on his day off to sign the paperwork. I was officially divorced almost four years to the day after my marriage began. What a wonderful judge to do something like this for me! God was watching over me!

*****

Why did I go through this? God knows, but I think I really needed to get to the point where having a human man was something I didn't need. I needed to stop expecting men to make me happy and just lean on Jesus.

I did know something else about myself—despite being in a bad marriage, I was never unfaithful. I could look back and know that throughout my relationship with Stony, I didn't do things I'd regret. I didn't compromise my faith. When Stony told me I had to choose between church and our marriage because church was a disruption (yes, he told me that), I wouldn't stop going to church. I would not let a man control me or make me do something I'd regret. I was true to God and I had peace.

I was more than happy to have a perfect man in my life and his name is Jesus. He will never cheat on me, He will never steal from me, and He will never forsake me. He will be a perfect husband and father. He never chastises but does allow me to suffer consequences so I learn with the goal to become more like Him and closer to Him.

Becoming more like Him is our goal and it is biblical, but it also warms my heart as I think about the couple that starts to look like each other as they get older. They smile like each other. They hold their heads like each other. It's wonderful. As we walk closer to God, I would love for someone to say, "You look just like Him!" What a compliment. I was going to choose to walk closer and have Him be my man.

CHAPTER 15

Husband #3

It was Christmas season the year of Stony's and my divorce when Heidi called and invited me to go country line dancing with her and her husband Ed and some of their friends. She says she can't dance well and I love to dance and Ed needed a partner.

I thanked her and told her no; I was busy.

She called me and asked me what I was doing. I told her I was going to my boss's house for a Christmas dinner.

She asked me what time.

I told her 6:00 p.m.

She asked me what time I thought people went to the bar dancing.

I told her I didn't know.

She told me, "Long after six—you're going!"

After an eye roll because it was not the time of my life that I wanted to go out celebrating and having fun even if it meant I could dance, which was a favorite thing—close to reading books, but not quite. As I thought about it, I remembered my good friend from church and the cute guy from church line danced there, so maybe it would be okay.

After the Christmas dinner, I went home and put on my country line dancing shirt and jeans. I got the shirt for $4.95 or some outrageous price and had never worn it, so it was a good excuse to put it on in public instead of leaving it hanging in my closet.

I always wanted to go to Bresa dancing, but Stony always told me I couldn't go because whores went there. Well, since I was a hoo-er for Halloween all those years ago, I guessed I'd fit right in.

I drove to Bresa del Rio to meet Heidi and her friends. They were already there when I got there. It was busy! Lots of whores around, I guessed.

I went inside and looked through the maze of people trying to find my sis and her friends. Finally, I noticed they were sitting right in front of me. I felt kind of dumb, really more scared and uncomfortable. I ordered a glass of ice water and tried not to feel so out of place.

Heidi asked me if the cute guy from church and my friend were there. I told her I hadn't seen my friend, but I said, "The cute guy from church is over there in that archway." I didn't point because Mom said pointing was rude—besides I would have died if he would have seen me looking that way.

Heidi looked over toward the archway and said, "Yeah, he is cute."

I soon realized that Stony and his girlfriend Jaime were there. It all made sense to me now—this is why he never wanted me to come here—it's where they hung out and having your wife and girlfriend at the same place probably wasn't such a good thing.

When I got up to use the restroom, Stony followed me calling me rude names that I won't repeat. I was scared out of my mind. I absolutely was not any of the names he called me, and I was here with my sister, not another guy. Heidi stayed close to me, and whenever I had to use the restroom, she put herself between Stony and I. Eventually he got tired of the game and left. I can't imagine what it felt to be Jaime going through that. I would have bolted.

After an hour or so, Heidi told me, "You know the cute guy from church has been looking at you all night." I looked over to where he had been earlier, and he wasn't there. I truly had not been looking; there was enough man drama to hold me for a long time.

I told her, "I don't even know where he is—how do you know he has been looking at me?"

She said, "No, he's still there. See, he's the guy in the blue shirt."

I told her, "The guy from church is wearing a white shirt, not a blue shirt." Then I looked back to the archway and saw the guy in the blue shirt. I told her, "That's not the guy from church."

She replied and told me, "Well, he's been watching you since you walked in."

I didn't know him, but the guy from church eventually did come and ask me to dance. It was fun—he was a good dancer, but he was a little crazier on the dance floor than I found comfortable. It does make me smile to remember him dancing. I decided he probably wasn't going to be the guy for me ever, but that's okay. I do think he is cute to this day and he now has a lovely wife!

Not too long after Stony left, Mr. Blue Shirt from the arches came and asked me if he could have this dance. Awww—he was so kind! I said sure.

He held me close, but not too close. He told me he noticed me because I couldn't find my friends even though they were right in front of me. When the dance was over, he escorted me back to my seat like a gentleman and told me thank you. He didn't call me any rude names nor did he treat me like a whore. I didn't see any whores that night—they must have all been hiding.

Later, Blue Shirt asked me to dance again. He smelled good. It was nice to be treated like a lady.

He asked me to dance every slow dance, and finally he asked me if I was available. I told him I was not. I explained that I was married and my divorce would not be final for two weeks. He said he appreciated the honesty and asked me if he could call me some time. I told him that would be nice and told him my phone number. The fact that he would likely not remember it as he had no pen and paper sprouting from the end of his arm didn't even matter. He had made an evening that could have been terrible a whole lot better. Sort of like Cinderella except I wore cowboy boots instead of a glass slipper.

The last dance I had with him, he kissed me. I thought I would melt into the floor. I couldn't help but notice that he had hair sticking out of the top of his white T-shirt that he wore under his blue flannel shirt. Even though Grandma Van said she didn't know how women could stand a man with a hairy chest, I told Grandma I could stand it just fine. Even just seeing that tiny little hint of a chest made me smile. Poor Grams didn't know what she was missing!

He gave me happy memories. Something to dream about after I went back home and I thanked God for giving me a nice gift for Christmas.

*****

Mom and Dad came home at Christmas and stayed at my house because I had a house and they didn't. It was still weird to think about them living in an apartment while Dad went to school.

When they were leaving, Dad gave me my favorite treasure I own.

I didn't have a special love in my life that Christmas except Jesus and He was a newborn so I didn't really expect the Christ Child to do the task of filling my stocking. I didn't think about my stocking—I'm not a person who likes getting presents—I'm the person who likes to give them. So my stocking hung empty from the mantle, and I think it made Dad sad. Before he left, he wrote a note and tucked it in my stocking. I found it when I took down the stocking to put away my decorations. I cried at his thoughtfulness. It said,

> Di's stocking was hung
> By the chimney with care,
> In hopes that someone
> Would leave something there.
> I searched through my pockets
> And the green suitcase too,
> Just had to find something
> Especially for you.
> "Time to get going!"
> Said Mom, with a shove.
> So I'll leave these three quarters,
> And my heart full of love!
> I love you,
> Dad
> '93

I have kept that note and those three quarters in my stocking ever since. They are the most special thing I own. If there was a fire and I had to grab one thing that wasn't living, it would be that stocking. I know the Bible says we are not to have a love of money, but I think even God will understand that it's not the value of these quarters I love, but the hands that put them there.

A few years ago, we had a family gathering at our house. I told my cousin Anne about it, and I was very tearful. She said, "Awww!" and got tearful herself. I looked across the room and found my dad had been listening. His eyes may have been glistening a bit too—just some pollen in the air bothering his eyes, I guess. For a dad who never expressed his love in words much, he sure showed me how much he cared by the things he'd do to make me feel special. I love you, Daddy!

*****

The days after the night at Bresa, there was no phone call from Mr. Blue Shirt. I'd just have to treasure the memories and the clean smell of his soft T-shirt. But I remembered that he had nothing with which to write my number and I wouldn't remember someone's number on my own.

But, on the third day, my phone rang and this sweet voice said, "Hi, Diane. This is Bill Barton. Is it okay that I called?" He told me that he repeated my number over and over in his head until he got to his car and could write it down.

He told me he didn't want to seem too eager, so he thought he should wait a few days. That made me smile.

He talked to me a long time—I hadn't talked to a guy on the phone like that since I was a young girl. It was really nice. He had a sense of humor. He told me he was interested in me because I was drinking water at a bar—I was a cheap date and could always be a designated driver. Nice! Nothing selfish about him—ahem!

He invited me to go to a New Year's Eve party that a guy at work was having, and I agreed to go. I was divorced now—barely.

I had a nice time. Bill called almost every day and talked to me until the day they disconnected his phone. Yep, I was long distance for Bill, and he hadn't paid his phone bill. I thought I'd said something or done something, but after his phone was reconnected, he had to explain. It all made sense to me the first time I went to his house. It was apparent by the pile of unopened envelopes on top of his refrigerator that bills didn't get paid when they stayed in the envelope. I think God needed to give me to Bill so I could take care of those things for him!

I was very concerned about the kind of person Bill was. He told me he had three girls and he was divorced. I was apprehensive. He didn't seem like the lying sort, but I had been through a lot. What if he lived in a dilapidated trailer with dead cars in the yard?

One night when I was talking to him, he said, "Excuse me a second." He put his hand over the receiver and yelled, "Girls, put your mattresses back on your beds and stop riding them down the stairs!"

Oh my stars—he had stairs! That means he didn't live in a trailer! I was so happy!

Now the alarms should have been going off in my head—Red alert! Red alert! Red alert!—he's raising unruly heathens who ride mattresses down the stairs! But I was so excited to know he had stairs that I didn't think through the sirens!

As much as I was content and happy with the thought of Jesus being my only man, I was enjoying my time with Bill and it was mutual. Within six weeks, I knew I'd marry him. That's scary, but he was not boring nor was he out of control. To quote Goldilocks, "he was just right." I didn't tell Bill that because the whole thought freaked me out, but my heart knew.

When we did talk about such things, I told him, "God talks to me. How do you feel about that?"

He asked me how God talks to me. I told him about God telling me I would be married three times. He said, "I'm good with that. He said three, not four, and I'd be number three."

Logical, I guess and he didn't bolt from the room at the thought.

He and the girls drove from Scotts to Plainwell to go to church with us.

He had identical twins—Becky and Betsy that had blonde hair and Jessica who had brown hair. Becky and Betsy didn't look identical to me at all, but lots of people couldn't tell them apart. I'd tell them, Betsy is taller and she has a "t" in her name. Oooh! They got that—unless the twins weren't standing next to each other.

Abbie liked them and it was nice because she was only three, so there was no competition for attention; they had different needs. They thought she was really cute, and she was. It was also nice because the twins are normal twins in that they're so close, they're like one person, so Jessi was left out. Even though Abbie and Jessi were six years apart in age, they had each other and that was really nice.

Bill asked the girls if we should get married and they were for it. But I told Bill, "I won't marry you unless God says."

He asked me, "How are you going to know? How will he say?"

I told him, "If God sells my house for $125,000, I will marry you."

He said, "But your house isn't even for sale."

"I know."

Bill, not to be deterred because he needed someone to pay his bills, went to Bob's Hardware and bought a "Home for Sale" sign. He made a wooden frame for it and banged it into my front yard. No phone number. No price. No nothing. Just a sign.

Two days later, a man knocked on my back door. He asked me if he and his wife could see my house. Sure. I let them in. They loved it. He said, "I'll give you $125,000 for the house." Okay, God! I am going to marry Bill Barton.

Note, Bill never asked me to marry him. I had been married two times before, and I always dreamed about these most romantic marriage proposals. Nope, I had once been proposed to in an entryway while putting on my shoes, another time when he came in from mowing the lawn, and then Bill—who said, "Why should I have to ask you when I know you'll just say yes."

I guess I am not going to live the Harlequin Romance life!

I was afraid to tell people—what would they would think—I hadn't been divorced for long. I started with my pastor. He had seen

Bill and the girls in church every week. He said to me, "Diane, I think this is wonderful."

I called Mom and Dad on the phone. Mom told Dad, "Diane said she's getting married to Bill." Then she told me, "Well, your dad's still sitting upright." Then she laughed.

No one seemed to freak out about it. It was kind of weird and wonderful all at the same time.

On August 8, 1999, Bill and I were married at the bottom of Bond Falls in the Upper Peninsula, four miles from the cabin Grandma Koehl's father built, my favorite place to vacation as a child. Dad performed the wedding ceremony. The girls carried bibles with flower bouquets I made tied on the top of them. The few people who were tourists visiting the falls that day thought it was absolutely wonderful! Grandma Koehl was there in her wheelchair, Bill's mom and dad and his brother and wife, and Heidi and her family were there too. It was small and it was special.

We were doing a lot of work on the cabin that week, so Bill and I stayed with all of the kids—including Heidi's two—at another cabin down the road. Very romantic—just Bill and I and six kids. The night we were married, Bill asked his mom if they could take the girls so we could have a night to ourselves. "Sure, honey!" she said.

The next morning at 7:30 a.m., his mom showed up bringing the kids back. She pounded on the locked door. We didn't answer. She yelled out, "What are you doing? Can you answer the door?"

Bill yelled back, "Mom, we're in the shower—it was our wedding night! Can you give us a minute?"

"Oh, okay!" she said and they waited outside rather impatiently for us to finish our shower.

I laugh because life with his parents was sort of like that!

Bill's house was on the farm on the opposite side of the country block from his parents' home. They would stop over often for a visit. I loved them, so it wasn't a problem except we were remodeling, and for about a year, our bedroom was temporarily right inside the door through the glass French doors.

We had the kids all the time and it was rare that we had any privacy. One weekend, we were actually alone—the kids were all elsewhere and we took the opportunity to "sleep" in. Sometime before 8:00 a.m., Bill's dad came in the front door.

I dove naked off the side of the bed opposite the glass French doors and crawled into our one and only bathroom. I quickly shut the door, closed the lid on the toilet, and sat atop the lid freezing to death.

Bill acted all cool and sat in the living room talking to his dad for almost an hour. His dad asked him, "Where's Diane?"

Bill said, "She's in the bathroom."

His dad said, "Wow—she's been in there a long time! Well, I'd better get going." And he finally left.

I was about unglued! I told Bill that he needed to lay down some ground rules with his parents! They were not to come over before 9:00 a.m. and they needed to knock! And we needed to keep clothes closer to the front room. And he had better get our bedroom upstairs done soon!

He thought I was being a little dramatic! I told him he could sit on the cold toilet seat and tell me how dramatic I was really being!

Haaa! Marriage is wonderful!

Well, it really wasn't for a while.

*****

Dad told me once that the problem with people today is they get married not realizing marriage is like a roller coaster. At the beginning of the ride, it's all uphill. It's scary because you don't know what's coming next and it can be so fearful that they get off before the "wheee!" He said people need to stay on and wait for the wheee!

I like that. He is right.

I knew one thing—God brought us together. I knew it. His signs were not coincidences. But, even when God makes something happen, it isn't always wheee!

I was not trusting. I was so afraid that Bill was going to be like Stony.

I am very thankful that as high-strung as Stony was, Bill was the opposite. Sometimes I felt I needed to check his pulse. I could scream at him with frustration and ask him if he was even "in there" because there'd be no response. He wouldn't fight back. He'd just take it. I shouldn't complain, but I told him communication means you have to talk, not just listen.

He'd say, "But I don't know how I feel about that. I need to mull it over." Sometimes I'd wait a whole day. Finally, I'd say, "Well, are you done mulling?"

He'd ask, "About what?" (Slaps head hard!)

I'd remind him and he'd say, "Oh, I forgot about that." (Slaps head hard again!)

We had a lot of conversations in the closet because it had sound-proofing and the kids couldn't hear me hitting his head against the wall. (Okay, I really didn't do that—I just wanted to sometimes!)

When I thought I couldn't take it any more—whatever it was—not just our communication styles being different because I really loved him, he would tell me, "My girls needed a Christian mom. Do you see Jessi in her room reading her Bible? That's when we know it's all worth it. We will get through it. God put us together."

Darn him. He was right.

As wise as he was sometimes and as much as he wanted a Christian wife, he didn't want to be a Christian husband.

He loved going to church in Plainwell, but after we got married, it was too far from his home. I knew it was important for the girls to be active in church. We needed to find something closer, so every Sunday, I would take Abbie with me and we would visit churches. Nothing seemed right.

I'd drive past a nice church not too far from our house, but it was an Evangelical Free Church. I'd never heard of that before—didn't know anything about them. Maybe it was a cult or something—so I kept going past it to other places further away.

One Sunday, I decided we'd go to that one. Weirdest thing (well, it was a God thing, but I didn't understand it at the time), Bill and the girls came too.

I walked in the door, and Bill's Uncle Ron, sweetest thing on the planet, was the greeter. He welcomed us and I got goose bumps. They (the goose bumps, not Uncle Ron) were zooming all over me—

up and down my arms and legs and they wouldn't stop. I have never ever felt this before, but I knew something—this was my place.

When we left church that day, Uncle Ron told Bill, "Billy, I hope you come back."

Bill said, "We will."

I tried not to trip or react too much. Then the girls said out loud, "We want to come here."

Oh God, you are sooo good! It was perfect! The church wasn't a cult. They took up an offering, so I wasn't exactly sure what the "free" in Evangelical "Free" Church was all about.

Bill worked a lot of overtime, which included some Sundays. A few weeks later, I got the girls up and told them it was time to go to church. They were really good and never back-talked me. When we got there, they asked me, "Are we here for early church or late church?" (because we had two services).

I told them, "Neither, we're here for Sunday school."

They weren't comfortable enough with me to give me smack about why they had to be there for Sunday school. I don't know that they even knew what Sunday school was, but I took them to their classrooms and headed to the adult class.

When it was over, they came running up to me and told me how much fun they had. We all went together to the church service, and later when their dad got home, they couldn't wait to tell him about Sunday school!

The next Sunday, they were all about going again. Bill told me, "I will go to church, but I'm not going to Sunday school. You take the girls and go separately."

I didn't want to push him—that doesn't ever work, so I took the girls and went. He showed up for church and I was just really thankful that he was there.

We were invited to a young adult group—they got together outside of church to hang out. I was sooo excited! I couldn't wait to go, but when it was time, Bill looked at me and said, "I'm not going. I have no problem with you going, but I'm not going to hang out with a bunch of freaks."

I was so hurt. This is the man God gave to me? I went alone. This was definitely the uphill part of the roller coaster ride—I was feeling no wheee!

In church they were talking about "Fire in the Woods." The church owned a decent amount of property and on Sunday night they were all bringing a dish to pass and roasting hot dogs on a big fire and singing songs. The girls and I wanted to go. Bill wasn't going to go because it was an activity with the freaks, but the girls and I would have a good time. I made my dish to pass and then my migraine hit.

I knew I needed to lay down and make it go away, but there wasn't time; we had to leave soon. I went to Bill and told him, "I know you don't want to go and I really want to respect that, but I want you to know that the girls are really looking forward to this. I made a dish to pass, and I would just like to ask you if just this once, you can take them. I promise not to ask you to do it again, but I don't want to disappoint them."

It was for the girls and he knew they were looking forward to it, so he said yes.

By the time they got home, my headache was gone. They had a great time, and Bill looked at me and said, "That was really fun." I zipped my lip.

The next week, the girls and I got ready for Sunday school, and when it was time to go, Bill was standing there dressed and ready too. I looked at him and asked, "What are you doing?"

He replied, "I'm going to Sunday school. Don't say a thing."

I smiled and didn't say a thing as we all got into the car as a family and headed for Sunday school.

God, You are so good. You give us the desires of our hearts. Proverbs 3:5–6 states, "Trust in the Lord with all your heart and lean not on your own understanding; In all your ways acknowledge Him and He will make your paths straight." I was definitely leaning on Him and He was holding me up! Thank you, God!

I know that God tells us not to be unequally yoked. Why? It causes frustration for sure. But, if we are or one of us becomes a believer, it doesn't mean we should divorce. God can use us, but I think it is very important not to drive our spouse away by our faith. We are to be an example that shines a light into their darkness. Light should be soft when we shine; we should never be like a hurtful light that my grandma used to be when she shrilly yelled, "Daylight in the swamp! And whipped back my bedroom curtains so the bright sunshine could burn the retinas in my eyes!"

God's time. God's way. Be patient and know that He is God. Nags don't draw people to the Lord.

*****

Not too long after we started going together as a family, the youth leaders left. They needed someone to help out. I felt God tugging at my heart. I loved being a youth leader all those years ago when Robert and I were first married. I really wanted the girls to be involved, so I told Bill I wanted to be a youth leader.

He was fine with it. Another man would help too. Bill could participate as he wanted, but I wasn't expecting him to be a leader.

The challenge was, in order to become a youth leader, we had to be members. It required us to meet with the elder's and share our testimony of faith.

We set a time and met with all these very godly, wonderful men, and I prepared my heart to be disappointed because I knew we had been married before; how would they take it?

I shared first because I had the most difficult past. Then Bill shared. He told them honestly that if he knew how hard it would have been on his girls, he would have tried harder to make his marriage to their mother work. He wasn't the person he was now all those years ago when they were divorced.

The men didn't berate us. They welcomed us into their church family with love. They could see our hearts and intentions, and they said not only could we be members but I could help with the youth.

I loved it! We just jumped into belonging to this new family who loved us immensely with no judgment—as God said it should be! It was a true church family. They asked me personal questions, not to gossip, but because they wanted to get to know me better. Many

117

people assumed Abbie was Bill's because she was so little, but I told them she wasn't and that her dad and I were divorced. I explained without hesitation what he had been like to me and that I decided I would not raise my child in a home like that, so I chose to leave. I remember the conversation with Sally and she kissed me on the top of the head and said, "I am so glad you are here. You are safe now."

Such unconditional love. Such forgiveness. God tells us to be this way to each other, but I never felt it so strongly until we were here in this place.

Our past is our past. It can never be our present because it's done. It's so much easier to talk about it freely and let God set it free like a balloon toward the heavens. I am free—free indeed (in a free church that takes an offering...)

*****

I haven't shared an animal story in a hundred pages...time for some more. It's been decades since the farm in Plainwell, so onto the farm in Scotts.

Cats

(1) Living in the country, it's a good thing to have cats—they keep the mice away. Bill's farm couldn't have had a mouse because he had lots of cats. Feral cats and cats named BJ.

The first-generation cat the girls had was called "BJ"—for Boots Junior. At a very young age, BJ had a baby that looked like her that the girls called BJ Junior. BJ Junior also gave birth to another kitten that the girls called BJ Junior Jr. Kind of like George Foreman's sons who are all called George? Because there are not enough names in the world to choose from!

When the girls told me their names, I looked at Bill with raised eyebrows. He just smiled and said, "Becky named them." Oh, that explained things.

The cats were all inbred and had an assorted number of toes on each foot.

One of the neighbors had a nasty cat named Oreo (because he was black and white—duh!). He was nasty, not because I don't love Oreos because I definitely do love them, but this Oreo would come over, enter the garage, and poop on Bill's stuff. I know why he did that—Bill hated him and he knew it. Why did he hate him? I don't know, but he did. We knew it and so did Oreo.

Oreo defecated one too many times on Bill's stuff in the garage and Bill had it—he went to the manure pile, pulled out the pitchfork, and shoved it through the side of Oreo and then put the pitchfork back into the manure pile, Oreo and all. Yes, an animal was harmed in the making of this book, but the statute of limitations has run out. Bill is not a murderer—stay tuned.

To Bill's shock, a few minutes later, he heard a clang as the pitch fork hit the cement. He turned around and the pitch fork was empty—Oreo had managed to pull the pitch fork off the manure pile, slide off the pitch fork, and run away. God (or Satan) spared him.

He did live—yes, for years. Never saw gangrene hanging off his body either. Maybe Dad was wrong. Maybe when I was a kid mucking Pawnee's stall with my bare feet, maybe I could have skewered myself and not gotten an infection. Maybe all the urine in it makes it sterile? Interesting!

I did tell Bill if I ever heard of him doing that again…

(2) Another time, the girls came running in to tell us they heard a kitten meowing from a hole in the floor of milk barn.

Bill and I went out there, and sure enough, a tiny screaming voice was calling from a hole that was a small three-inch drain pipe into the floor.

I was frantic. Hysterical! We had to get the kitten out!

Bill, who you have learned is not overly sensitive, looked at me and asked, "What do you want me to do? Break the floor apart?"

What did he think I was going to say, "Yes!" Of course, he should.

He proceeded to tell me that was just dumb because it was only a kitten and the cat would surely die in the process. But I told him he had to do something.

Enter Bill Barton the muller. He mulled hard, but not long enough this time to forget why he was mulling...besides I was standing there ringing my hands and hopping back and forth from one leg to another, so he had to mull more quickly than normal. Then he said, "Get the shop vac."

What? Why?

"Do what you're told and go get the shop vac—now!"

I did it and with horror watched as he removed the end of the hose and shoved it down the hole.

I was screaming, "Nooo! You can't suck the kitty up with that!"

He said, "It won't go up the hose—it'll just get its head stuck. It'll die in the hole or it'll be deaf, but it'll have a chance."

"Oh God—this is awful!"

Flip—on went the switch, the vacuum roared to life, Bill yanked on the hose, and up came the kitty.

Miraculously, she sat there looking fine, like this happened every day.

I never loved and hated that man more in my life—he saved the kitty. Her eyes were still set properly in her head and she seemed to be able to hear. But he could have killed her (unless she had more than one life like Oreo).

(3) The girls were always playing with the kittens. We had fresh ones born all of the time, so they were good entertainment.

One time after an especially hard rain, I was out in the yard after the sun came out and I heard more meowing. This time it wasn't coming from the milk house but from over by the front horse pasture. As I got closer, I saw a big blue fifty-gallon plastic barrel with a piece of wood over the top. The crying seemed to be coming from inside.

I lifted off the lid and found six baby kittens standing on their back legs with their faces peering just above the water line.

I freaked! I did a lot of freaking when the Barton girls were around, I think!

I reached down and grabbed them out as fast as I could. They were all fine, but I don't want to know how long they were in there.

I rarely ever yelled at the girls, but this is one time I didn't wait for their dad to discipline them. They promised they'd never put kittens in fifty-gallon barrels again. I breathed. They lived—both the kittens and the girls.

(4) The farm had lots of barns with old junk in them. I'm slightly (or majorly!) more tidy than Bill. I was always picking up pieces of wood and putting them on a big pile on the cement pad between the barns so I could burn them when winter came.

Winter and snow came, and I decided it was probably safe to burn it. I was home from work with pneumonia and was feeling a little bored. So I got some newspaper and a match and lit the pile.

In case a spark blew off, I stayed and watched like my dad always told me to do. I wouldn't want one of the old barns to catch fire.

About an hour into the inferno, from the center of the pile came a smoking ball of cat. How it stayed in there the whole time, I don't know. It was singed but seemed fine. Oh my goodness! I don't think I wanted to be a cat on our farm!

Draft Horses

I wish I had draft horses—they're my favorite. I think they are absolutely incredible. They are so muscular; their hooves are huge. They are magnificent!

Our neighbors who went to our church, Russ and Ruth Bartholomew, had a pair.

They asked if we would mind if one day they could pick Abbie up from the neighbor's house after school and take her for a wagon ride. Seriously? Of course!

Russ and Ruth were the most God-fearing people I knew. If I died, I wanted Bill to marry their daughter, JJ. She is very sweet. Then, Abbie would be able to truly keep Russ and Ruth as her grandparents and I don't think you could get better than that.

Every time I saw Russ, I'd say to Bill, "I love Russy." He'd smile and say, "I know."

Russ was an elder at our church. If he had been alive in Jesus's time, he would have been one of the twelve, I'm sure.

One time, after Bill had finished building our bedroom (after the episode of sitting naked for an hour in the bathroom), Russ stopped by to see Bill about something, but Bill wasn't home. I was so thrilled about my bedroom, I asked Russ, "Would you like to come up and see my bedroom?"

He chuckled softly and without making a face, he said, "Sure."

I showed him what Bill had done and he told me what a nice job we had done with it and then it sank in—I just asked Russ Bartholomew to my bedroom! I was horrified! I said, "Oh my gosh—Russ—I asked you to my bedroom!"

He smiled and said in his very soft and quiet voice, "I know, but that's okay. You were just happy to show me what you did. It's fine."

Bill thought it was a hoot, but not as big of a hoot as what was going to happen next.

The day came when Russ and Ruth took Abbie for a wagon ride. When we got home, Abbie came running from the house and said, "Grandpa Russ and Grandma Ruth came and got me on the wagon and we went to Hooter's!"

Bill looked down at her and said, "What did you say? Where did you go?"

She said, "We went to Hooter's and got ice cream!"

He lost it—he asked her, "You mean you went to Scooter's for ice cream?"

She said, "Oh yeah, Scooter's."

She had no idea really what Hooter's was, but Scooter's was the little ice cream shop a couple of miles away.

Bill couldn't resist calling Russ and saying, "So I hear you took our daughter to Hooter's! Russ, I don't think that's okay!"

Oh poor Russy—he was so embarrassed. Then he said he thought it was so cute that she got that wrong.

God doesn't make guys any sweeter than my Russy!

Goats

When Grandpa Russ found out that Abbie wanted a miniature goat, he said they had some and he would bring her one.

I think I was more excited than Abbie because goats were one animal that Mom refused to have on our farm. She said they were stinky, but they're not if they're fixed. Mom wouldn't buy it, plus I think she was done fixing animals.

I thought goats would be a good thing to have because we could tie them out and let them eat the grass.

Bill didn't argue and he got a doghouse for the goat, and Abbie was over the moon when Russ brought him home to us.

She named him Billy Button. She had to—we have two names in our family BJ and Bill—my grandpa was a Bill, my dad is a Bill, my brother is a Bill, my husband is a Bill, my father-in-law is a Bill, so we needed a goat named Bill too. My Grandpa Bill used to sing me the song about Bill Grogan's goat, but I don't think Abbie knew that song, so he came about the name "Billy Button" quite innocently. Mom, however, said, "Couldn't she pick another name?" Ha! Nope!

Living in the country, it is totally acceptable to bring your goat to show-and-tell, and Abbie did. He was so cute. I loved the little guy, but he didn't live too long.

Russ felt so bad. We're not sure what happened to him. But my Bill had nothing to do with his death. There were no pitch forks involved.

Poor Billy Button. Note: We never replaced him with a Billy Button Jr.

CHAPTER 16

Everything I Have Comes from Him

When we come into the world, we don't bring a purse, a wallet, a small personal item that we can store under the seat in front of us, or a carry-on that must fit in the overhead bin.

Everything that comes to us afterward is truly, I believe, a gift from God.

We don't get to pick our parents—God does that.

We have a lot of other choices in life that we do choose—our mate, or in my case, the herd of them, our friends, our church, our job. I believe God puts people in those places and I believe he blesses us with open doors.

One thing God talks a lot about in the Bible is money and our treasures. A lot of people get really squeamish when it comes to money—a "It's mine! Mine! Mine!" keep-your-hands-and-your-minds-off-it attitude. I feel very different about money. I think it's truly a gift. I think God has a huge influence on who gets what and I believe He watches what we do with it.

I absolutely believe God gave the world enough of everything to go around; He just didn't evenly distribute it. Reminds me of how my beloved Bill spreads his creamy peanut butter onto his bread. It's just the perfect amount—not too much to stick in the roof of his mouth and it must be enough to go all the way out to the edges. It makes me insane to watch him spread it—it takes way too long if you ask me. I asked him if his mouth really knows it's exactly the same depth all the way around. "Doesn't it just matter how much is in the bite you put in your mouth?" He says no. I just don't think it's very efficient.

Second Corinthians 8:14–15 says, "At the present time your plenty will supply what they need, so that in turn their plenty will supply what you need. There will be equality, as it is written: 'He who gathered much did not have too much, and he who gathered little did not have too little.'"

I think our job is to spread it around when we're given a larger piece than everyone else, and I think God watches us to see if we're "Mine! Mine! Mine!" Or it's "ours."

When I became the treasurer at church, I went to a Christian financial conference, and one of the speakers shared this statistic, "If every *Christian believer* tithes, within five years, there would be no more starvation or lack of clean water in the world. Plus, there would still be enough money to support all our clergy, missionaries, and churches.

I found that profound. How is it possible? Because the average believer only gives 2 percent.

God gave us the answer in his book. How can God not take care of everyone? He did—we didn't! We aren't sharing. We aren't behaving like His hands and feet. It's a call to action, not an injustice!

I frankly know I have been blessed. Blessed to receive, but more importantly, blessed to have the privilege to be God's Santa to the rest of the world. It's my greatest joy to share *because* when I share, I start with a shortage. What God puts on my heart to share is not what He puts in my cup. If I need to share eight ounces, He gives me two ounces *at a time*, but He keeps refilling it.

It requires an act of faith for me to pour out the two ounces and not keep some for myself, but over and over, I've watched God provide a beautiful fountain—like a glorious heavenly waterfall of the most soft, pure, clear, amazing water imaginable! But if we keep it, that two ounces get a dirty film on it after a while. It starts to stink and rot and pretty soon, it isn't fit for me to keep either. Because of our untrust, even what we had is taken away because we hoard it.

I challenge you to dump it out; get fresh; every time He shows you some person or organization that needs watering. Then set your cup down and let Him refill it. Trust Him, He will!

Compassion

Eight years ago, we were in a small group Bible study and we were reading "Crazy Love" by Francis Chan. I was so moved by the book and how Francis had been downsizing his worldly possession to focus on what is really important—Him, not things.

I remember one day I was home alone, which didn't happen often. I was sitting in my chair in my living room with my feet propped up on the ottoman, and I had the thought, "You've really done well for yourself." It was as if God smacked me upside the head and asked, "Really?" No sooner than I thought it, I regretted it. I know everything comes from Him, and I never wanted to be able to have a thought like that again!

I prayed to the Lord His prayer from Matthew 6:9–13:

> 9 This, then, is how you should pray:
> Our Father in heaven,
> hallowed be your name,
> 10 your kingdom come,
> your will be done,
> on earth as it is in heaven.
> 11 Give us today our daily bread.
> 12 And forgive us our debts,
> as we also have forgiven our debtors.
> 13 And lead us not into temptation,[a]
> but deliver us from the evil one.[b]

I told God, "I want to rely on You for my daily bread. I want to know that I can't make it financially through a day or a week unless Your hand is in my life."

I knew I wanted to give away "my" money such that the only way I could live was trusting Him.

I already had four Compassion kids and one World Vision child, so I said, "God, if I sponsor fifty, there is no way I can afford that. So I'm going to do it and trust that You are going to care for me!"

I started crying—not because I was scared but because I felt overwhelmed by the Spirit. It was such an emotional moment with God—one I'll never forget. I couldn't wait!

I got my laptop, and I started searching Compassion's website for children—trying to find the countries where they had children that were the most impoverished. I picked one child after another until there were forty-five new children I could call my own. Then, unfortunately, I stopped. It was so exciting yet so sad. There were so many more that needed sponsors...

Bill came home a while later, and I told him what I did. Bless his heart, he never flinched. He'd seen God take care of us over and over again, but I expected more of a reaction. He just said, "Okay," and went downstairs to watch TV.

The first thing I was tempted to do is figure out a way to budget this in, and I had to remind myself, "No, this is God's thing—you need to trust!" But I did feel I needed to help Him out a bit. So I stopped putting money into my 401(k) except the little bit of money that my company would match. God didn't tell me to do this, but I was sure He needed me to help a bit!

The other thing I worried about is how I was going to write to fifty kids! So I went to my friends and family and asked for help writing. I kept six, and I arranged for forty-four correspondent sponsors to write letters for me. The hard part was they would never know I was their sponsor, but that was selfish—it wasn't about me.

When I told my mom what I did, she did what most mom's do and worried enough to take one of the kids from me—the one I had chosen because he shared her name. But that's not what I told God I would do—I said fifty, not forty-nine, so I had to get another one!

Three months later, I was amazed to find that I had extra money in my checking account—the amount equal actually to what I had would have put into my 401(k). So I said, "Okay, God. I guess you have this covered. I'll put into my 401(k) again," and I did.

It's been eight years now, I think. There's not been a time when the money for the kids hasn't been there. There's never been a time when I couldn't pay my bills. I can't explain it in human terms—it isn't possible. Well, but it is possible. Every month, God provides my daily bread. Every month, He makes sure my children are sponsored.

Plus, Compassion now has a program where I can write letters online and upload pictures and copy a letter over to send to another child, so even though my friends and family haven't always been able to write, now my children all get regular letters.

I've gotten quite attached to the kids. Sometimes they share very personal things with me—one of my favorite boys told me his dad had a mass in his chest, but he couldn't stop working to have the surgery because he needed to work to support his family. I called Compassion to find out how much money I needed to send to make sure he could have the surgery and not work. They couldn't answer me—they just said whatever I would send would be enough, so I sent extra money as a family gift. It sometimes takes months to get answers to letters because of the time for translation back and forth, but months later, I did get a letter from Aldrin. His father had surgery and he was fine. God provided again—for the money for the surgery and for his father's healing. Thank you, Jesus!

One little girl, Madeline, told me she really wanted a cow so they could have fresh milk. I called Compassion and said, "I need to get a cow for Madeline." The lady chuckled politely and told me that I couldn't get a cow for her. I could send a family gift, and the Compassion person in country would work with the family to purchase whatever the family should have because what if I got her a cow and they had no way to feed it. I had to trust, but I really wanted her to have that cow. A few months later, I got a picture in the mail attached to a letter from her—she had a cow *and a goat* and the neatest thing ever—she was smiling. In her country, the children do not smile for photos (like we used to have somber pictures in the US), but she was smiling ear to ear! God granted her wish and mine.

I wasn't ever going to talk about the Compassion kids, but a couple of years into my sponsorship, I received a call from a man from Compassion. He asked me if he could come and talk to me. He said, "You are sponsoring fifty kids. I want to hear the story."

I agreed to meet with him. I told him what God had done. He asked me, "Do you ever talk about it to anyone?"

I told him, "No, the Bible is clear that we are to give such that the right hand does not know what the left is doing."

He said, "Diane, I want to challenge you to think about that. I understand what the Bible says, but what God did for you is a miracle. People would be inspired by what He did for you. I think you need to share His miracle."

I did understand what he was saying—to not share is like hiding Him under a bushel and not letting people see that He is alive; He still performs miracles. But I do guilt well and I want to obey, but I trusted this man—I didn't think he would try to lead me to do something that God would disapprove, so I share His miracle of what He did for me.

I met with him again and he brought me a gift—a widow's mite. It is in a little wooden box and it is a genuine coin from Jesus's time. Yes, of course, I cried when he gave it to me. Again, a treasure of mine that is money, but it is not the currency itself, but the story behind it that makes it one of my most special things. I didn't give all I owned as the widow did in the story, but I did trust God to provide for me as she did, but how the woman in the story touches me and how he touched me with his little box and the coin inside!

> [41] Jesus sat down opposite the place where the offerings were put and watched the crowd putting their money into the temple treasury. Many rich people threw in large amounts. [42] But a poor widow came and put in two very small copper coins, worth only a few cents.
>
> [43] Calling his disciples to him, Jesus said, "Truly I tell you, this poor widow has put more into the treasury than all the others. [44] They all

gave out of their wealth; but she, out of her poverty, put in everything—all she had to live on."

God gives us the desire of our hearts. He gave me mine. He gives me joy. He provides for me. But He asked me to open my hands and my heart so He could use me. I am so blessed. Am I surprised? No, God is very clear…

> [7] If anyone is poor among your fellow Israelites in any of the towns of the land the LORD your God is giving you, do not be hardhearted or tightfisted toward them. [8] Rather, be openhanded and freely lend them whatever they need. (Deut. 15:7)

> [17] If anyone has material possessions and sees a brother or sister in need but has no pity on them, how can the love of God be in that person? [18] Dear children, let us not love with words or speech but with actions and in truth. (1 John 3:17–18)

> [21] Jesus looked at him and loved him. "One thing you lack," he said. "Go, sell everything you have and give to the poor, and you will have treasure in heaven. Then come, follow me.
> [22] At this the man's face fell. He went away sad, because he had great wealth. (Mark 10:21–22)

> [10] Give generously to them and do so without a grudging heart; then because of this the LORD your God will bless you in all your work and in everything you put your hand to. (Deut. 15:10)

Can I eliminate world hunger? No. Can God? Yes, but I believe we are the hands…

I am not asking all of you to tithe. That's a personal decision you need to make, but God is clear! What I am asking you to do is trust God to give you this day your daily bread, and when He does, slice a piece off the loaf and share it with someone else. Remember the miracle of feeding the five thousand? I think He can still do it!

Bill Gets His First Refill

Not too long after we started attending Country Christian Evangelical Free Church, it was obvious that the church was growing and they wanted to add an educational wing on to the end of the church. I really wanted to be a part of this because it was exciting and our youth would have more room.

They started a capital campaign and asked for pledges. I felt God telling me to give an amount—I don't remember exactly how much it was—I just wrote a check. When God tells me to give, it's the one leap I will just make trusting Him. I told Bill, "He always provides."

The next month, our credit card bill came due. I didn't have the money to pay it off in full because I'd given the gift to the church. Yes, I know, I could have paid more the next month, but it's absolute heresy to pay interest! I was really frustrated about it when my husband, the newbie to this faith thing, said to me, "Why are you worrying about this? You are the one that told me He always comes through if He tells you an amount to give."

I said, "But I'm $850 short! I don't see how He is going to do that!" Bill looked at me like I'd sprouted a unicorn horn and just walked away.

That week, we got a check in the mail for $850 for overpayment of our mortgage escrow. Incredible! Like that happens every year—like never before or since in my life! And the amount wasn't a coincidence. When God makes a statement, He makes it loudly and He shouted this one at me. It was amazing for Bill to see God in action doing the thing He does when we obey.

M-I-S-S-I-S-S-I-P-P-I

We heard about a mission trip to Mississippi to help with the Hurricane Katrina victims. The purpose was to build a new home for a single mom and her two boys whose house had been destroyed when a bus landed on their house during the storm. Unreal.

Bill is an amazing builder, so these types of things allow him to use his talents to give back. I love to use my hands as well, so I was excited to help.

We went to the first meeting and found out that the couple that was going to cook was going to be unable to be there the third of the four weeks. They really needed someone who could make meals. Cooking is my passion, and even though I really wanted to run a screw gun for the week, it's probably safer for Bill's sanity and the plumbness (that's not a word, but I'll use it anyway because I like it) of the wall that I take responsibility for this other need. They were thrilled! It had been a big worry for them and God just checked that off the list.

It was going to cost $1,000 each to go on the trip. We didn't have the money in our checking account, but we knew we were supposed to go, so we signed up. The Compassion miracle had happened shortly before so we were definitely living on faith and not a healthy bank account.

I made food ahead—for some reason that God new about and I didn't (yet), I made a huge number of pans of lasagna and put them in the freezer.

We had been really busy at work. The FDA had given us a warning letter that affected labeling, which touched my department. My wonderful team of employees and I had been making a lot of changes to how we did things, and we were getting remarkable results in a very short amount of time. I was so proud of everyone. The change was hard, but it was really good and we were rocking it!

I had been working a lot of extra hours but somehow managed to get to the planning meetings for the trip.

I got an appointment for a meeting in the ECR later that day. I had never heard of the "ECR." I looked at the other names on the appointment and they weren't people I normally worked with, but I started calling and emailing people asking the location of "ECR." No one replied. I missed the meeting.

About an hour after the missed meeting, I got a response. The ECR is the executive conference room—the place where the big boys meet in the corporate office. I had missed a meeting with the CEO. Oh my—that's not good. I blew it kind of badly, I guess.

The executive secretary who had called me apologized for assuming that I would know about the ECR. She told me to come over later that day, so I did. It was just me and the CEO.

I probably looked scared to death, but he smiled and shook my hand and gave me a check for $1,000 to say thank you for the hard work I put forth during the recent crisis. They saw the effort and appreciated it.

Wow! God is good all the time. His timing is perfect. The amount was not more or less than I needed. It was exact, no waste!

When we got to Mississippi, things went well. I figured out my kitchen digs and got into the routine of making all the meals.

A couple of days into the trip, we learned there was a horrible accident. A small boat had capsized in front of the place we were staying—they couldn't find survivors. Divers were called in and the family members of the people on the boat were standing on shore. We could see them. It was right in front of us, and we were heartbroken for them.

One of the leaders on the trip came to me and asked, "Diane, I know this is a lot to ask, but I just went and told those people that we would like to feed them dinner. They're not leaving the shore and they are hungry. Is there any way you can feed them?"

Oh God, you are sooo good. He knew ahead of time what would happen and He prepared me for it. I had the ridiculous amounts of lasagna that were not made by accident and all I needed to do was put the pans in the oven.

When I told him I had enough food already, he couldn't believe it! But we could believe it. His plan is perfect and his plan is complete, and I got to watch him unfold it. Blessed!

CHAPTER 17

Homes

When I married Bill, I still had my place at Sandy Pines and my house in Otsego. You know I sold my house for $125,000 as a sign from God to marry Bill, but Sandy Pines was my only remaining possession from my life before Mr. Blue Flannel Shirt. I loved the lake.

Bill's girls were shy and even though there was so much fun stuff for kids to do at Sandy Pines, they didn't like it. They complained when we went there. I'm a firm believer that having things/toys are okay as long as you use them but not if you don't. That to me is hoarding—perhaps a different kind of hoarding, but hoarding none-theless, and God could be doing something else with that money.

So, with sadness, I put Sandy Pines up for sale. I got $50,000 for it. I was all in with Mr. Barton because all my premarital assets were basically gone—except Abbie, but she wasn't to the age that I wanted to sell her to the lowest bidder yet.

I was driving around on my way home from work one day and drove in to Lake Doster. There was just a pull; it's not like I ever did that, but that day, I did. My journey led me to a spot at the back of the lake that was undeveloped and there were for sale signs on some lots. I was drawn to it.

I came home and told Bill what I'd done. He said, "I can't believe you did that without me." He seemed a little perturbed. I felt badly—I didn't mean to exclude him; it just sort of happened.

The very next day, we got a packet in the mail from the realtor with information about the lot. I looked at Bill and asked him, "How did this happen? I didn't ask for this and I was just there yesterday."

He laughed loudly (I love his laugh) and said, "I was there the day before you and I called the realtor and asked for the information."

"You turd!" I yelled and slugged him in the arm. "You made me feel so terrible!"

He said, "Yeah, I know. It was pretty fun."

We made an offer on the lot but found out it had sold the day before—the day we had been there—the day the realtor had sent us the information. But the lot next to it, that was three times bigger for the same price, was for sale. We bought it.

It had lake access, so I basically was trading one lake property for another. I felt good about it. One day, Bill would build a home there for us. I was so blessed.

We put the farm up for sale. I had reservations, but it was one hundred miles round trip for me to go to work every day. I was tired of the drive. The twins were old enough to drive now, so every other weekend when we had them, we could pay for their gas to come half-way—it would be a lot easier on me. I had been making the trek for four and a half years and Bill said it was time. Even though we would still go to our church, that was only two trips a week, not five, and the two trips were half what I was driving then.

We had done so much work on the farm. It was beautiful. We stood to make a lot of money on it, and we could use that for materials for the new house.

We got an offer! It was from a lady moving from Connecticut, and she wanted immediate occupancy upon closing.

So we looked for somewhere we could stay while we built the new house. No apartment was going to house us and four kids. We finally decided we would buy a small house and sell it once we were done with it. We found one in downtown Plainwell. The couple that owned it was wonderful. We fell in love with them right away.

Mom and Dad were living in the UP, but they had come down for Grandma Koehl's eightieth birthday. It was a quick trip—Dad had to get back to preach on Sunday. My mom has to be in on everything. So, when she knew we were going to buy this little house, she was all excited about it. On the way back north, they got off the highway at Plainwell and peeked in the windows. Four hours later, they called us when they stopped halfway at the "bridge" and said, "We want to buy that house! When your dad retires, we want to move back to Plainwell and we love it. We'd like to live there. Can you rent it from us instead of buying it?" Was she kidding? Yes!

To make room for the new owner of the farm, we moved out and into Mom and Dad's rental home. All was great. Bill started building our new home—everything was falling into place.

Until the farm sale fell through.

We now owned a farm, were paying rent on a three-bedroom house, and were building another home. Nooo! How would we manage?

We separated off three and half acres of the farm and lowered the price.

We got an offer. Relief.

It fell through again.

Bill continued to work full-time on the new house. It was exciting, but it was scary. Our funds were dwindling. We had taken out a home equity loan on the farm and we were maxing it out, and I was nervous. I still had to pay the bills and we were getting deeper in debt.

In casual conversation, I asked Bill, "If I can't take care of myself someday, will you take care of me?"

He quickly replied (without mulling at all), "No."

I was shocked. I looked at him and said, "Really? You wouldn't?"

He said, "No. I couldn't really do that."

Oh.

Three weeks later, Bill was in horrible pain. He couldn't walk. I had to help him while he leaned his full body weight on me to try to walk him to the bathroom. Then I had to unzip his pants and help lower him to the toilet. Dear God, what was happening?

He looked at me and said, "I think I'd like to change my answer." Yeah, I bet you do, buddy!

He went to a rheumatologist, and they had him take Ibuprofen and did tests to see what was wrong.

In the meantime, we were trying to do as much to the house as possible before winter set in. So I took a week off work and went to the job site with him. The plan was he would sit in a chair and tell me what to do. We were forming the exterior of the house with ICF (interlocking concrete forms), so it was something I enjoyed—it wasn't a traditional stick-built home. He felt pretty good in the morning, but by 3:00 p.m., we had to pack up and get him home while he could still walk.

They diagnosed him with reactive arthritis. They believe he picked up a virus in Mexico when he was on a mission trip. The virus was gone, but his body thought the fluid in his joints was a virus and his body was trying to fight off something that was no longer there. They put him on injections and it worked to suppress his immune system and allow him to function again. Thank you, God! The other praise is, unlike some forms of arthritis, it doesn't harm his body or joints; he just has to be careful not to be around sick people because the medication doesn't allow him to fight off even a cold very well.

So Bill was back to work on the house without me.

All was good until one day I told Bill, "You have to stop building. We literally have $25. You cannot buy a bolt, a screw, a nothing. We are done!"

That day the farm sold. This time, the sale did not fall through.

God's timing was perfect again. We didn't need the money yet. He gave it to us when we needed it—when we could no longer rely on ourselves but had to trust in Him because we were beyond our human means. Plus, the people that bought the farm eventually asked to buy the three-and-a-half-acre parcel, too, and we ended up getting more for the whole farm than we ever thought we would, so God provided abundantly.

Eve and the Fire

We loved our years at Doster, but living in our neighborhood were a very few but very powerful neighbors who liked to tell us what to do. It finally was too much for Bill to handle. We made some of the best friends we've had in our adult life, but it was time to move on. Bill wanted to be back in the country with privacy and the ability to do whatever we wanted without people making up rules and harassing us when we wouldn't follow them.

I was heartbroken, but I know there were many, many days that I would sit in my living room and look out the back at the waterfall and the marsh and be amazed beyond belief that God let this simple girl that grew up on a hill a few miles away live in a magnificent home like this that husband #3 built with his very own hands. He was incredible and I never took it for granted even one moment. But I knew, it was just a house—it was a shelter; it was not what defined our family, but rather was where our family lived…for a time.

I started looking for homes online. It took a long time before I found a house I liked. I told Bill I wasn't selling my dream house until I found something I liked. The home he had built for us was just so wonderful. He understood.

One day, I stumbled across a home in Paw Paw. It was really pretty. It had stone on it like Grandma and Grandpa's and my house—except it was fake rock, but pretty. It sat in the woods and the inside looked nice. I don't know. I wasn't sure. I felt God would call me to it when the time was right.

I looked at the pictures that same house over and over for months…wondering but not moving forward.

Finally, I decided to take a drive by "on my way—not!" home from work. I really liked the outside. The setting was beautiful. I came home and told Bill, and he said we could take a look at it. It was for sale by owner, so I called the lady and we went to see it.

When we got out of the car, she came up to me and she said, "It's you, isn't it? I've been praying for God to send me someone and I think it's you."

I looked at her and shook my head and answered her, "I think so."

She hugged me. Bill tossed up his hands and said, "I don't even know why I'm here!"

It wasn't perfect, but we both really liked it. We made an offer and they accepted. We closed on November 1. Because I knew it wouldn't take long to sell our house, we didn't want to get a bridge mortgage or anything. We used the equity on our Doster house and

0 percent credit cards (lots of them) to come up with the money for the home in Paw Paw. We wouldn't have to pay any interest for eighteen months, so there was really no risk. I know people cringe about using credit cards but 0 percent is 0 percent. Yes, it would affect my credit rating, but only temporarily. I wasn't going to need a loan, so what did it matter?

I moved my plants there right away upon closing, so I wouldn't have to move them when our house sold in the winter. I didn't want them to die from the cold.

We were excited—now we could sell our house. We put it on the market and waited for someone to buy our home that was absolutely wonderful.

And we waited. And we changed realtors and lowered the price.
And we waited. And we changed realtors and lowered the price.
And we waited. And we changed realtors and lowered the price.

We'd had five people tour the home in one and a half years. The feedback we heard was that it was the nicest house they'd seen. No, it wasn't overpriced. It's just not what they wanted. No one was coming… I knew I was to thank God in advance for what He was going to do and I was thanking Him, but it was like, "God, are you home?" Silence…

Abbie called me frantic. The house where her best friend from Lake Doster had lived when they were kids was burning. His parents still lived there. Could they stay in our house that was for sale? "Yes, of course!"

Abbie took them her house key. They were so happy. Their house was a total loss. There had been a train on the tracks in Plainwell that blocked the fire trucks from getting through quickly. By the time they arrived, the house was engulfed. The firemen went through breaking windows and tossing pictures outside onto the lawn—their treasured gifts—memories of years past. They ran out in their bare feet saving the dog, but the cat was nowhere to be found.

After the fire was out, the firemen found the cat. She was okay. She hid when she got scared, but miraculously, she would live. Another cat, another life!

They now had a place to stay—somewhere close to home so they could sort through things, meet with insurance agents, wash smoke-filled clothes, lay their heads, take a shower…they were so thankful for open doors.

Our home had a purpose and I was finally at peace about our house not selling. God needed it for our dear friends, and I was okay with that! More than okay.

It was right before Easter when all this happened. The Allens had planned to have Easter with family at their house—and they did; it's just their house was our house. There were beds for everyone because the house was furnished so it would show well to the five families that saw it in one and a half years.

The day before Easter, it was cold. Missy Allen was home and there was a knock at the door. She opened it only to find a small girl and three very large dogs standing outside. The little girl and the dogs were lost. They were wet and covered with mud. The little girl wore no coat even though it was frigid.

Missy put the dogs in the garage so they wouldn't run off and brought the little girl, who said her name was Eve, into the house. She was cold, so Missy took off her wet clothes and put them in the dryer and wrapped her in a warm blanket.

She asked Eve where she lived. She said she and her mom were visiting her Aunt V. Aunt V lived in a house with a barn on a very long driveway. Eve's mom drove a red SUV, but she didn't know the address.

Missy immediately put a note on the Lake Doster Facebook page asking if anyone knew of a family that met these descriptions. Incredibly, Bill and I were eating lunch and saw the post. Bill said there was only one house in Lake Doster that had a long driveway and a barn—it was a half mile away.

I replied to Missy telling her what Bill said. The police were out scouring the neighborhood for a red SUV and Missy let them know they should check out this house. They did; Eve did not come from that home. So where did she come from?

Missy asked Eve if she was hungry. She said she was; she hadn't eaten yet that day—it was after noon.

Missy gave her some cereal.

Eve told Missy that she had gone outside to play with the dogs. Somehow, she had gotten turned around and before she knew it, she was lost. She said she had been walking a long time, but she wasn't scared because the dogs were with her. She went on to say that she had come from the dead end, and when she got to the road, she prayed to Jesus and asked Him which door to knock on and He said, "This one." And that's what Eve did.

Eve trusted Jesus to show her where to go. He didn't leave her as she came cross-country! The dogs were by her side and she had not come from or through the neighborhood!

Missy let the police know that she had come through the old golf course—hundreds of acres of wilderness, which explained why she was wet and muddy.

The police said they had been called before to a home with three dogs that matched the description of the dogs that were with Eve, but it was miles away. Could she have walked that far?

They went to the home, and indeed, Eve did start there and her mom and Aunt V didn't realize she had been missing. We believe she had been gone four hours. Eve was seven years old.

Eve's mother and Aunt V followed the police to our house. They stood outside taking for about fifteen minutes and finally went in to get her and take her home. Unreal and scary.

One hour after Eve was retrieved, our realtor called and we had an offer on our house.

God was done with it. His plan was complete. Eve was home. The Allen's stay would be completed in a week. It was time.

I shook my head. I couldn't have imagined how His story for our home would unfold.

The zero percent interest for eighteen months on my credit cards ended in two weeks. God was in no rush; it was all okay. Seriously, God, I think you like to watch me sweat buckets? *Heavy*, sigh!

CHAPTER 18

Family

Grandparents

I was blessed to have my four grandparents into my thirties. I know that isn't typical, and I am so thankful that God let me keep them as long as He did!

All my grandparents were special in their own way, and I will treasure the many memories I have of them.

Grandma June was the last one to go to heaven. She always seemed very young—and she was. She had my dad when she was only twenty and he had me when he was twenty, so she was as young as some of my friend's parents. She was really beautiful and she and grandpa were very in love with each other. She was an avid bowler and golfer. She once had a hole in one. I called her my young grandma.

Grandpa was very special to me. He died of Parkinson's, and Grandma was alone on their farm. Grandma's friend died of colon cancer and she was horrified of getting it because her friend's death was so horrible. So, when Grandma started passing blood, she was sure she had cancer. She didn't go to the doctor to find out; she just ignored the signs that something was wrong thinking if she didn't face it, it would not be real.

I went to visit her one time and noticed a blood trail down the hall. It was cause for concern. We made grandma go to the doctor. What they found is that she had diverticulitis, not cancer.

Unfortunately, she had lost so much blood in the time she was avoiding her symptoms that she suffered a stroke. In an instant, Grandma June went from being young to very old. She was paralyzed on her right side. Suddenly she went from being an incredibly talented artist focusing on her gift of oil painting, to not being able to lift a paint brush.

One thing that didn't change was her spunk. She had to live in assisted living and eventually in a nursing home—living twelve years after her stroke. She was a favorite patient of the staff because of her sense of humor. They called her the sock lady because she loved bright holiday socks. There was no need to label her clothes; no one wore anything like Grandma June!

At the very end of her life, her memories were gone. They were trapped somewhere deep inside of her brain, and she didn't recognize us anymore. Her body was just a shell. Dad went to visit her on his birthday. He asked her, "Mom, do you know what day this is?" She replied, "Of course, today was the day you were born!" It was his special gift. No sooner had she told him this than she was gone again—to that place where Grandma went inside herself when she no longer was present with us. But no one could take that away from him. Beautiful! Thank you, God!

Grandma June was the first family member I knew that wanted to be cremated. When she died, it was sad, but we said goodbye to the spunky lady so familiar to us a year before. Parting was sad but beautiful; we knew she was in heaven with her Savior.

Because many of her family members were away for the winter, we decided to wait until summer to have a memorial service. Since it was months between her passing and her service, time had healed our hearts somewhat. There were many friends and family that came to share memories. It was truly a wonderful day.

After the gathering, a smaller group of close family went to the cemetery to place Grandma's ashes in the ground next to Grandpa's casket.

There was a small square hole in the ground. We carried her ashes to her final resting place in the cemetery and Dad performed the graveside service.

Eddie, age eleven, Heidi's youngest, always likes to wear a suit. He looked especially dapper that day. Dad looked at Eddie and asked, "Eddie, do you want to dump Grandma in the hole?"

Eddie looked pleased, surprised, yet touched to be asked and answered, "Sure."

So he took the lid off of the box and started dumping Grandma in when a swift breeze suddenly picked up and Grandma blew all over Eddie's nice suit.

Eddie looked rather startled—a little afraid he would get in trouble for doing something wrong. What does a polite young man do with Grandma all over the front of him? Nothing really prepares us for a moment like this.

I'm sure Grandma did this intentionally—she always was the one to do something no one expected—why should today be any different?

Seeing Eddie's concerned face, Dad said, "Just brush her off into the hole, Eddie!"

Eddie did.

The once sad moment ended in hysterical laughter from everyone present! That's my grandma!

Stepmom

When Stony ended up marrying his mistress, I was definitely not okay with Abbie being around her. This was the woman who destroyed our marriage.

But, a few years after they were married, I realized something. Stony wasn't truthful. I didn't break up his previous relationship; Stony did. He actually picked out some pretty wonderful women— why would Jaime be any different?

As Abbie went to visit Stony, I began to be thankful that Abbie wasn't alone with her dad; Jaime was there. She was a mother to her own children; she would take care of Abbie too.

God had turned my hard heart into a soft heart. I began to love this woman.

Abbie told me Jaime wasn't her mom. I told her that she was her mom, and it was okay for her to call her mom because she was her stepmom and I was sure she loved her. It made things much easier for Abbie and honestly, for me too.

About four years after Bill and I were married, I thought about her and realized she could be going through some hard times herself. What if Stony treated her like he did me? What if she was ever afraid? I was fortunate that I had a very good job and a house and a place at Sandy Pines when I met Stony. I could get away. What if she had no place to go?

I called Jaime. I told her that if she ever needed a place to go, she could come to our house. Stony would never look for her at our house; she would be safe.

She was definitely caught off guard, but she thanked me.

I will say that this strength to call her was definitely not a strength I had on my own; I know that it was a strength and a drive that came from the Holy Spirit, but when I obeyed Him, it was the most incredible feeling to love someone that I didn't know I would ever love; and it was deep and it was real.

She has never showed up at my house, but the offer will always stand.

The longing of my heart is to go on vacation with her some-day—to thank her for all she did for me by loving my child when I couldn't be there for her myself.

The other woman can be—and in my case, was—a gift from God. Thank you, Lord, for Jaime!

CHAPTER 19

Children—Aren't You Proud?

There are people, like my mom and my daughter, who want to grow up and be a mother. Children are their dream in life, their human fulfillment.

My dad and I, I think would like to admire them from a distance, but we are filled with some kind of kid catnip that attracts them even when sometimes we'd rather just put out a bowl of food and check on them in a week.

If I'd never been able to get pregnant, I think I would have lived, but I would have truly missed out on some incredible stories that I will treasure in my heart forever even though I didn't always appreciate them in the moment!

I'm so thankful for Stony's parents and their decision to watch Abbie when she was little. I have fond memories of their house and how they accident-proofed every corner that she could accidentally bump her head on as she toddled around. There were red clown noses and folded up washcloths duct-taped everywhere. It was a little over the top, but no harm should come upon her in their presence.

Because she was so spoiled, Pawpaw would drive to Burger King every day and buy her a Filet-O-Fish patty because that's what she wanted. But in case she could choke on the breading, he used a very sharp knife to filet the breading from the patty. Quite ridiculous, if you ask me, but I said not a word. Let me clarify, I am not exaggerating—he drove there every single day, Monday through Friday for years! Had they not heard of frozen fish sticks? But for the princess, she only needed to utter the wish, and they would grant it!

As a by-product of all of this wish granting that they did for her, the word *no* is something she also wished would be struck from her kingdom's vocabulary. Unfortunately, the evil biological mother and stepfather were not so easily swayed by her whiles and did she make us pay!

I Think I'll Just Brush My Teeth Now

When Abbie was eight, we learned that her mouth was too small and her teeth were nice sized and she would not have sufficient room in her mouth for everything if we didn't go through the process to expand her jaw. My cousin Anne, who is a dental assistant, put us in touch with a wonderful orthodontist in Grand Rapids. He fitted her with an expander, and we went every month for appointments. Every day, Abbie turned a key in her mouth to make her jaw bigger.

We decided it would be a great treat to take all the girls on a family event to 5/3 Ball Park to watch a baseball game. The morning of the ball game, disaster struck and Abbie fell off her bike and skinned up her knees in the road. The disaster was small and we washed her up, but I felt bad for her—I still remember the throbbing sensation of doing that to myself decades earlier. Their baby skin is so soft and fragile!

The game was pretty fun. I don't think the girls watched it, but they consumed a grossly expensive amount of food and found some friends they knew. I'm not confident they even realized there was a ball field—just a bunch of people and food.

On the way back, Abbie fell asleep. By the time we got back to the house, the car was pretty quiet. The sugar had worn off and it was time for bed.

I went in and headed to the bedroom to get into my pajamas. The big girls headed downstairs to watch television for a bit.

Bill carried Abbie from the car to the house, but when he got to the doorway, he was worried he would bang her tender knees on the doorframe, so he set her down and told her to go in and brush her teeth and turn the key in her expander.

The minute her feet hit the floor, she started screaming. She didn't want to do all of that—she just wanted to go to bed, but she had eaten insane amounts of sugar, so she just really needed to do what she was told.

Because she wouldn't stop screaming, Bill picked her back up and took her out the front door and stood her on the large landing step right outside. He turned the porch light on and told her that she could come in once she got herself under control.

Not being so obedient, I guess Abbie decided that getting herself under control must be predicated by a running and screaming session around the front yard unmatched in volume to a comparable eight-year-old howler monkey.

Since we lived in town and it was after dark, Bill decided that it would be prudent to fetch the squalling child and bring her inside. He took her back into the garage and sat her on a pile of mattresses that had come from Grandma Van's house. Grandma had recently died and we had moved some of her things to this house.

As Abbie sat on her comfy throne, Bill perched on the top of the freezer and they talked about whether all of that was really necessary. She had calmed down by now, and it appeared everyone was going to survive until Bill saw flashlights in the windows in the top part of the garage door. Soon the police were pounding loudly on the garage door. Oh no!

Abbie, sure that someone was coming to get her, screamed loudly once again and came running into the house, through the kitchen, and downstairs looking for me. The girls told her I wasn't down there, and they didn't know where I was so she came running back upstairs.

At the sound of her screams, the police officer who was posted outside the front door came bursting in at the same time Abbie reached the kitchen. She screamed again yelling, "Please don't hurt him! He didn't do anything!"

Now, for the first time since I had been home, I realized something was going on. I had been getting ready for bed at the other end of the house. Abbie's screaming was nothing new as tantrums were a regular part of her eight-year-old life, but "Please don't hurt him! He didn't do anything!" What was that all about? There was only one him in our family, if you didn't count the dog, and he was pretty old, so I was quite sure he wasn't the "him" she was flipping out about.

I came down the hallway in my nightgown to find my little girl and a man with a gun in my kitchen. I sat down in a chair, and Abbie came running over to me leaning her whole body into my side. I asked, "What is happening here?"

The officer said, "That's what I'd like to know!"

Abbie quietly answered, "I wouldn't brush my teeth."

Yeah, he wasn't buying it. He said he was going to talk to his partners.

About that time, we heard laughter coming from the garage.

The two officers that came into the garage when Bill pushed the garage door opener wondered the same thing. Bill explained what had happened, and they were cracking up. The one officer said, "When I was her age, my grandma put me in the snowbank in my underwear when I had a tantrum." They saw the humor, but the officer from the house did not.

He told me if they got any further calls, they would be investigating and we would not get away with it!

Yes, we'd had three squad cars circling our house!

When they left, Abbie looked up at me and in a very quiet voice said, "I think I'll go brush my teeth now."

The girls came up from the downstairs when the coast was clear. They said, "We're really glad our mom lives in the country. If the cops came every time we screamed, they'd be there all the time!"

Yes, it was a bit of excitement. The girls were thrilled to share about the cops' visit during Sunday school the next morning. Abbie was horrified, and we had a little explaining to do to the church elders. Thankfully, everyone thought it was pretty funny except Abbie. She said she'd sue me if I wrote about this in the book, so please don't tell her you've seen this!

The PS to this story is many years later, Abbie was with her high school friend. The friend's dad was going to drop her off at our home. She told him, "You can just drop me at my grandma's house. It's closer than our house and Mom can pick me up on her way home from work."

She steered him to Grandma's house and he said, "You know... I was at this house years ago. There was this little girl who was screaming."

Abbie sheepishly replied and told him, "Yeah, that was me. I wouldn't brush my teeth."

I think he asked her if she does now and she told him she did. Ha! It cracks me up that she admitted it was her.

Threats!

Bill and I definitely do not parent the same way—especially when it came to Abbie. I know she is not his biological child. I know she pushed his buttons like a masterful accordionist, but the man who typically has the patience of a monk didn't when it came to her.

He made ridiculous threats when she didn't mind him. It was often a subject of our closed-door meetings in the closet. I told him, "You can't say such crazy things to her—she knows you don't mean it, so you need to stop. You are not going to do any of those things to her if she doesn't mind you. She needs to have consequences that are real!"

So the next time we were all in the car heading toward town and she got really sassy with us, which was literally about .4 miles from our driveway, he said, "Abbie, if you don't stop talking like that to your mother, you're going to have to ride in the trunk!"

I gave him a look to remind him of his recent private lesson. Not good—he smirked back at me.

She kept it up and he pulled to the side of the road and pushed the trunk release button and told her to get out and get in the trunk.

She said, "I will not!"

Then he told her, "Then I'll put you in there." And he did!

Yes, I was frozen. What in the heck?

Now, let me explain, I drove a Buick Park Avenue. The trunk could have held half of a soccer team. The only thing in it was reusable grocery bags and it was always clean. But it was still the trunk!

She laid down and he shut the lid. He got back in the car, put the car in gear, and drove off.

I stared at him with my mouth hanging open.

He laughed. He said, "She isn't going to die in there. I won't go far!"

Except…a car came up behind us and he couldn't pull over.

He turned off on the next road and the car followed…it happened again and again until he was literally probably three miles from the house. Now he was regretting what he did because he was a little scared—he just wanted to have her in there to carry out the stupid threat he made because I told him he couldn't do it—not like he really wanted to put her in the trunk (okay, I'm sure he really wanted to, but…).

He got out and opened the trunk. She looked at him and said, "I'm not getting out. I like it in here. It's clean and I can breathe. Besides there's this little lever on the inside I can pull if I want to. I'd rather not be up there with you and Mom."

Pushing his buttons in the key of C she was! Strong-willed does not being to describe… He yelled at her, "Get in the car!"

Realizing that perhaps this had gone far enough, she jumped out of the trunk and got in the back seat.

It was a quiet ride to town.

A Southern Son-in-Law

Abbie went to college at Abilene Christian University in Texas. She wanted to get as far away from us as possible and Texas was pretty far from Michigan. She and I went to visit the school, and if she didn't go there, I wanted to quit my job and attend; it was amazing!

I saved all the child support money from her dad for her education. ACU had a program where I could pay a flat fee for the year and she could take as many classes as she could all year round. It was possible that she could graduate in three and a half years and I would have enough money saved so she would only have to pay for the last six months out of her pocket. Cool beans.

151

Despite her desire to get away from Bill and I, by parents' week-end in October, she begged for me to come and see her; I couldn't—I had a charity event that we had been months planning and I couldn't change it at the last minute. She asked, "Can Bill come? I miss him!"

Wait, Bill? Bill—the throw-her-in-the-trunk Bill? The Bill she despised? Yes—apparently, the same one.

When she asked him, he paid for his own airfare and hotel and flew down to spend the weekend with her. They went to the football game and out to dinner together. He said it was the most wonderful time he'd ever had with her. I'm really glad I couldn't go or they wouldn't have had this special father-daughter time.

In the first semester, Abbie met a boy from Houston. He moved back to Houston and she was miserable without him, so after she finished her first two semesters, she convinced me that she wanted to go into a two-year medical program as either an x-ray or ultrasound technician. Since these are both amazing choices, I was okay with her leaving ACU and transferring to a junior college in Houston.

I rented an apartment for her, but after a few months, the relationship and her interest in school fizzled. I was not going to support her just living in Texas and not going to school, so I told her I was going to come down and retrieve her and her possessions and move her back to Michigan.

In the months between the break-up and the time I came to get her, she met another young man, Matt Johnson. His family was originally from Georgia, but his dad was in the military and was currently serving in Texas. I got to meet him when I showed up to load her things. He seemed so nice and she was going to break his heart. She said she didn't think she cared about leaving him behind. But on the drive back, they talked every hour. By the time she got to Michigan, she was despondent about being away from him, and two weeks later, Matt moved to Michigan and into our basement.

Abbie pushed him around a lot, and Matt just took it. Bill often asked him, "Matt, is that your spine hanging on the coat rack? Do you want me to get it down for you?" Matt would just patiently smile. How did she find such a tender, kind, and patient young man to offset her spunk? I guess they have them in Texas!

By summer, they were getting married. We told Matt there would be "no backsies." If he took her, he had to keep her. He said he loved her and we were so happy about having him in the family.

They got pregnant right away and blessed us with the most darling little girl that is the axel that her Papa's world spins on. Me, I may just like her a bit, too. Under two years later, Auggie was born and we have one of each. Because they love kids so much, they also do foster care. I love their hearts and I think they're crazy.

They're poor and often frazzled. They live in a very small house with three dogs, two cats, a guinea pig, two biological kids, and up to two foster care kids. When they get new babies, Matt, the guy who gets up at five thirty in the morning to go to the gym before work, will often walk the babies in his arms until they stop screaming and fall asleep and again. I think there must be angel wings somewhere under his shirts because I don't know how he puts up with the chaos, but he does and we are blessed.

I volunteer for Wings of Hope Hospice and the Wings Home—two amazing nonprofit agencies who provide care for the dying. Because they put patients first and the care they provide sometimes isn't fully covered by Medicare, Medicaid, or private insurance, they have to fundraise to cover what they need. The community is wonderful about giving and showing their support—the organizations are very loved.

This year, they decided to hold a raffle. The tickets were $50 each, which isn't cheap, but the winner got to choose a vacation trip to Maui, Riviera Maya in Mexico, or the Kentucky Derby.

I decided I was going to buy a ticket for Matt for Christmas. I didn't buy him anything else because I knew God was going to give him the trip.

I told Amy Chestnut, the coordinator of the raffle at Wings of Hope, "This is the ticket that needs to win," and I told her why he was deserving. She laughed and being the cutest thing ever, said she hoped that worked for me.

They sold just over five hundred tickets and the winning ticket would be drawn by the chief of police who wasn't going to buy a ticket just in case his name was drawn. The big drawing was held in a local restaurant, and there were perhaps thirty people that showed up to watch the chief.

I parked and walked across the street to the restaurant thanking God in advance for drawing Matt's name because I was just sure He was going to do it.

When I got into the restaurant, I noted that the chief is big—I wouldn't mess with him; that's for sure!

Amy asked me to spin the handle on the screened barrel holding the hundreds of blue tickets. I gladly did—it was fun; she told me she'd been spinning it all afternoon. She wanted to make sure that the last ticket sold wasn't on top. Then the chief spun the handle and I stood right next to him watching in eager anticipation as the tickets folded over and over on top of each other. Then, he stopped spinning and reached his huge hand in through the small opening and pulled out the lucky stub.

I looked over and briefly saw the handwriting thinking maybe it was mine. I mean, it was possible—I think it was black ink. Did I fill in my stubs with blank ink? I don't know. Then I heard the chief's deep voice say, "Matt Johnson!"

My eyes got huge, and I put my hand over my mouth and looked at Amy whose eyes were wide and her hand went to her mouth, and in unison, we screamed!

Everyone there looked at us like, "Who is Matt Johnson?"

I yelled, "I need to tell you the story! I need to tell you the story!

So, with rapt attention, they listened to me tell the story about Matt holding babies and working hard to support his young family.

With teary eyes, they told me, "I'm so glad you told us the story and I'm glad I didn't win if it means that this young man can take his wife for a week to paradise!" Yes, God, you are amazing! You give me the desires of my heart always—sometimes at the time I may not know they are the desires of my heart until later—maybe years later, but you take care of every detail and I think you like to give me joy!

Amy and I face-timed Matt. He was smiling so huge—it wasn't Christmas yet, so he didn't even know about his one and only present waiting under the tree—the other half of the raffle ticket.

Abbie was screaming in the background, "Is this for real or are you joking?" Amy said, "Abbie, it's for real!" More screaming!

Then, with a cute smirk on his face, Matt said, "Okay, I have one question. Do I have to take Abbie or can I take my mom?"

Smack—we saw Abbie's hand hit his shoulder hard as Matt laughed.

We told him he could think about it, and as his eyes twinkle, he said, "Okay."

What an amazing Christmas! In February, they went to Riviera Maya. They shared an adjoining room with us and they were able to take the little ones. Nana and Papa got to babysit a little so they could spend time out to dinner alone. God is good! All the time!

Thank you, God, for all that you do to supply wonderful new members to our family and for miracles!

Horses

To say that a girl likes horses doesn't fully describe how Bill's girls—especially the twins—felt about them. They were consumed with horses.

VHS movie cases held movies, sure, but they didn't care—they wanted movies so they could turn the cases on edge and make stalls for their Breyer horses. We had more Breyer horses than silverware.

I could not figure out why Becky had a little hole in the front of the collar on all of her T-shirts. Then one day, I realized that is where they hooked the leash that was her lead rope. Abbie was small so she rode her around on her back sometimes, but when she dismounted, she had to hold on to the "horse" so she wouldn't run off.

They played for hours!

They told me when they grew up, they were going to raise horses. They were going to train them. They were going to barrel race. I thought it was cute. A girl should have her dreams.

I doubted that it would ever amount to much besides holes in a T-shirt though because we had a horse and the girls were petrified—I mean petrified to get on her. Because they wouldn't ride, Bill eventually sold the horse to a lady who lived down the street.

155

When I was dating Robert, I used to dream about having a boy and a girl. The boy's name was going to be Joshua and the girl's name would be Becky. I was pleased that Bill had a Becky. She was so cute and she completed that fairy tale dream that hadn't come true the way I thought it would when I was a teen.

Those blonde jokes that everyone thinks are so horrible (that I think are funny, so call me twisted—my hair is blonde…at the moment anyway)—they are true. I know they're true because I have watched Becky and she does those things!

One day, the girls were playing in the yard. There was a deck off the side of the house and the sliding glass door opened up into the kitchen. I watched Becky come running to the house for something. She ran fast, clambered up steps, and ran full speed into the sliding glass door—bonk! She took a step back and twitched for a second and then seemed fine.

I asked her, "Are you okay?!"

She calmly said, "Yeah—I didn't know that door would be closed."

I replied, "Isn't it always closed?"

She said, "Yeah, but I thought today it might be open."

I told her, "Maybe you should check next time."

"Yeah."

After Becky moments like these, I would look at Bill and say, "Aren't you proud?" She was hysterical! Stinkin' innocent and hysterical!

Another time, we were driving to the Upper Peninsula to vacation at our cabin. The drive was long—ten and a half hours normally—fourteen hours with Becky in the car because thirty minutes after we'd leave a rest area, she'd push on her tummy and say, "I think I may have to pee again!"

We'd say, "Stop pushing on your stomach!"

She'd reply, "Well, I have to know if I need to pee!"

"You'll know!"

And she'd keep it up and we'd have to stop again and again.

We weren't too far into the trip—maybe an hour—when we hit construction. There were the typical construction signs, and Becky was looking out the window practicing her reading skills, "Ped-a-strain-eee-un." Yeah, "Pedestrainian".

No, we said, it's pronounced "Pedestrian."

"Oooh." Then quiet.

All of a sudden, she pipes up, "Injure/Kill Worker $7,500? Do you know how much money I can make if I injure or kill a bunch of them?"

My eyes got wide and I heard Jessica say, "Dad, aren't you proud!"

Becky says, "What?"

Bill went on to explain to her that you don't receive $7,500 for injuring or killing a worker, you have to pay it.

"Oooh!"

God help us! It's a good thing she's cute. God will need to make sure she marries a nice guy who can walk her through life because oh my word!

Are You His Babysitter or His Date?

One of the challenges of being is a girl is developing before boys. I remember going to school with the girls and I'd be so excited to have them point out to me the boys they liked. They'd talk about them all the time and doodle their names on their papers.

The whole little girl crush thing was wonderful and I was truly tickled about it.

They were super excited to show me so and so! But when they did, I was stunned. The girls were taller than me—they wore size 10 shoes, and these boys weighed about twenty-six pounds and were naval height.

I'll admit—I don't always have self-control when it comes to my mouth and I really feel badly about some of the things I've said, but especially when I asked them, "Are you babysitting them? I'm sure their mothers appreciate the extra help! Do they pay you by the hour?"

Bill would tease them about it too, and they would giggle and say, "Nooo!"

The Hair Dye Must Have Helped

At some point after high school, Becky dyed part of her hair darker for a time. I'm sure that's not the reason for the change, but there was a change nonetheless and I'm so proud of her and Betsy.

When her mom remarried, they had the financial means to really get into the horse business. They and their mom actually do raise horses. They have been successfully barrel racing for years and even hold events on her farm. I think Becky has something like seventy horses (they are in real fences—she doesn't use VHS tape cases anymore). She breeds the mares, collects sperm, and does ultra-sounds. She's incredible!

Betsy is in the business too, but she has to balance the horses with her time she spends with our most wonderful two grandsons, Jayse and Logan. She is an amazing mom. Betsy is married to a wonderful guy, Dustin, who is such a good family man and provider. He is a handsome guy—he doesn't weigh twenty-six pounds and isn't naval height. They deer hunt together and everything—pretty cool!

The Last Dance Is the Best Dance

Being divorced with children is so horrible. Bill loves his girls so much, but when he decided to end his first marriage, he really could not fully comprehend the sadness that would be his to bear over the years. Yes, he got off before the wheee!

I think God blessed both of our families despite this decision and I'm so thankful for Bill, but he has grown up and become more wise and appreciative.

Before his girls liked boys, Bill was their man. I remember when we were first married being amazed that Betsy would sit in his lap and snuggle him when she was fourteen years old. I asked him, "How long do you think she will do that?"

He said, "I don't know, but I hope forever."

When Dustin came into the picture, things changed. It's by God's design that she couldn't stay at home with her daddy forever, but it broke his heart. Nothing was the same after that; she was breaking away.

When Betsy was planning her wedding to Dustin, we were so happy for them. We wanted to be part of her special day, but clearly this was something she was planning with her mom and stepdad. Bill offered to help pay for it, but we heard nothing. It hurt, but not as much as when Betsy came to Bill and said, "I need to tell you that Mom and Ben are paying for the wedding and Mom said I am going to do the first father-daughter dance with Ben. I'm not going to have a fight with Mom. I do want you to both walk me down the aisle."

He was crushed, but he also understood that he loved her too much to put her in a bad place with her mother. He would just step back and be glad to have the part in her day that he could.

Her wedding to Dustin was beautiful—it was in a garden setting, but they had a covered place for the reception and there were clear sides that could drop down in case of rain…and was there rain!

Just before the wedding was to start, a front came through. It was fast-moving, but it was a lot of rain. I was so proud of Betsy because she said, "Maybe we should have the food first and the ceremony after? Can we do that? Is there a rule that the food needs to come after?"

She was so laid-back about it all, and since everyone was there and under cover, we just decided to wait it out. When the rain passed, everyone wiped off the wet chairs and it continued—just as planned, but a little later. No worries! Go, Betsy—no Bridezilla here!

When the meal was over, it was time for the father-daughter dance. Ben and Betsy took the dance floor. There were looks from the people in attendance. Everyone knew who Betsy's real father was and it wasn't Ben. Even her mom's sister asked Bill, "What the heck is going on? You should be out there—you're her dad!'

Just hearing the whispers and the comments not so quietly whispered made him feel better. He had taken the high road.

His turn with her came and people settled down a bit.

But then Betsy did something that I will cry about my whole life. They announced, "Will Stewart Johnson please come up?"

Stewart didn't know why he was asked to come up until he got to the dance floor and Betsy asked for a dance. I lost it.

Amy Johnson had been Becky and Betsy's best friend in high school. She came to youth group with them every Wednesday night. She was beautiful. She had a quiet temperament. She was soft-spoken and kind. Her heart was so sweet. We loved her! We can't always choose our kid's friends, but I think she was handpicked for us.

Amy had been going to school to be a nurse. It made sense—her personality was such a fit. She hit a patch of ice on the way home one day and her vehicle spun around, and she hit a tree and died instantly. We were heartbroken. She was such a loss. Why, God, why? Truly only He knows, but the pain was deep.

Betsy knew Stewart would never have a dance with Amy, so she gave him his own special dance.

He later told us if he had he known what she was going to do, he would have never come to the wedding. But she caught him off guard and he had no choice. She danced and loved him through it as he cried for the dance he would never have with his beloved daughter.

I bawled. Everyone that knew who he was had grabbed a napkin off the table. Those who didn't know his identity were asking, and through our tears, we shared the gift she was giving and more napkins were snagged.

Bill said, "It doesn't matter what order I danced. Stewart's dance was the most important." I don't think we could have been more proud of his little girl and her choices about what is most important in the dance of life.

After Amy's death, her parents started attending our church. I think Amy gave her parents the gift of faith. Would I die if it meant my family would know Jesus? I think yes.

They sat in front of us every week.

After we moved to Paw Paw, we changed churches. It was really hard—we love our Free Church family so much, but we visit on occasion and it's such a homecoming.

It had been a while since we'd been back, and we managed to steal the chairs where we always sat behind Stewart. He turned to me and hugged me and with tears in his eyes and a quivering lip, he said to me, "I need to thank you for what you did for Amy. She loved coming to youth group with you and I know where she is today because of you."

This friend's father has brought me to more mushy tears than I can count. His presence in my life has blessed me richly. Thank you, Lord, for your perfect plan even when we don't always understand.

Girl of Steel

Jessica, aka Jessie/Jessika/Jessiwatha/Jessissippi, now she is going by Jessi (Jessiwatha and Jessissippi are names she hates that her dad calls her to annoy her and it works), is our daughter with the strongest faith in Jesus.

It is Jessi that Bill pointed to when we were first married, and I didn't know if I was strong enough to be a mom and told me I was there for her.

When she was moody, she would go up to her room, lay in her bed, and cover her head with the blankets. When she would ignore me, I didn't know what to do, so one day, I went to the kitchen and got the salad tongs and came back up pinched her through the covers.

The blankets started shaking and she asked, "What are you doing?"

I replied, "Getting you with the tongs!"

Why? I don't know? It's stupid, but it made her laugh.

After that, when she was in a snit, I'd ask her, "Jessica, do I need to get the tongs?" and she'd laugh and tell me, "No!"

I have premonitions a lot and I don't like it. I always know what I'm getting for Christmas. I know when I'm going to be proposed to (or not).

When Jessi was twelve, I had the feeling that she was going to die. It was a horrible thought. I held it in never uttering this for years. One day I told Bill and I wish I'd never said it out loud, but there was a day I told Jessi too.

Jessi came to live full-time with Bill and me when she was sixteen. Her mother was struggling with her and we wanted her; perhaps a change of domicile would be good for her.

She got a job working at McDonald's in the drive-through. She was really good at it—she was a great multitasker. Plus, they let her take home all the leftover pies.

We bought her a little car to drive back and forth to work. She had to pay the insurance and gas, but we bought the car. I don't think she had much money left after she paid for the car expenses, but it was enough to buy cigarettes.

She'd sit in her room, open the window, and blow smoke outside—I'd find the butts and ash in the window and beside her seat in the car.

She definitely was rebellious, but to us, she was always kind.

We knew something was up, but we didn't know exactly what. We bought a tape recorder that connected to the phone so we could record calls and we put it under our bed. Maybe it was illegal, but we were taping our own family and we needed to know what was happening with her so we could help her.

Bill doesn't cry—at least I've never seen tears come out of his eyes very often—he gets pollen in there, he says, but the pollen just makes his eyes water—it's not enough to run down his cheeks—usually.

But, one day, there was a recording that changed that. Some boy had called Jessi and she told him that her dad had threatened her with a gun. She said Ben, her stepdad, had intervened. The tears ran down Bill's face. This never ever happened. The fact that she was telling someone he did this was awful...and why? So they would give her a place to stay and she could move out.

She was caught by the police at a party where she shouldn't be.

We knew we needed to take her car away, but she would be furious. But we couldn't let her just go and do whatever she was doing.

Bill made a copy of her car key, and we planned the day that he would go to school and take her car. We would put it at someone's house, but she wouldn't have wheels. She was going to be furious, but we were desperate to slow her down.

The day that we planned to take the car, God intervened. She was still in our neighborhood when her car broke down. She was halfway out of the development when it chugged to a stop, and there it sat alongside the road. God had done the dirty deed. Jessi helped

Him by not putting any of the twelve quarts of oil in her trunk into the engine like Bill told her to do because her car burned oil. For the first time ever, I was thankful for a toasted car!

Jessi moved out and dropped out of school. We called her school counselor, and she said if we could possibly convince her to stay in school for two and a half weeks, she would have the credits/classes she needed to graduate. She wouldn't do it.

She told us she didn't want to do things against the rules in our home because she respected us too much. Because she wouldn't follow our rules, she was choosing to leave.

Because she was seventeen, authorities said there was nothing we could do. We were distraught.

I had to practice what I described earlier and lay her on the altar and let God take her. It was so hard, but we had to trust Him—we had no other choice.

Jessi did at some point get her diploma, but she had to attend an alternative school.

She moved from house to house staying with other people doing things I don't care to know about, but drugs were her life.

She ended up in jail a few times. It was hard, but we wouldn't bail her out. It's horrible when you know that jail is safer than houses where there are drugs and people who use. We just kept her on that altar and prayed.

At one point, she was released. She came and stayed with us for a very short time. When she was there, I told her about my premonition. She smiled and told me, "It's okay, S'mom—I won't die." (Her name for me—stepmom, but she said that was a mean name and she didn't like it, so S'mom was better.)

The in and out of jail continued for years. We visited her a couple of times in different homes where she'd be living. It was always scary—we knew the situation wasn't good, but we loved her. I couldn't have loved her more. It was a lesson of unconditional love. I told her once I couldn't love her more if she was a princess in a castle on a hill—and it is true!

One day, Jessi was on the news. She was picked up in a raid. Eventually, she went to prison—the best thing that would ever happen to her (her words, not mine).

She ended up finally in a prison in southern Indiana right by the border. She was sentenced to three years. The place was beautiful—I would have wanted to visit if it wasn't for the fence and barbed wire. I'd never been to a prison before. The workers were friendly. We had to sign in at the gate. We could take in quarters for the vending machines; we could get her food during the visit, but we couldn't touch her—we could just sit across from her in chairs.

Another inmate asked if we wanted a picture together. Yes, but I was crying because I was inches from her, but I couldn't touch her. If I did and we were caught, it would be bad for her. The inmate looked around as if to see if maybe I could just touch her hand, but Jessi told her no. We understood—people could pass drugs. Jessi wanted to be clean.

She was in the dog ward. She cared for dogs that stayed right with her. She loved it.

She looked beautiful. It had been a long time since I had seen her sober. She was the Jessi from half her life ago.

She loved the workers and the warden. They were kind to her, but she was doing all the right things.

The warden arranged for any of the girls who were interested to go to college. She jumped at it—she was going to become a certified welder. They took a bus to school for weeks, and she got not only one certification but two.

The warden set up a graduation—complete with a motivational speaker. He was amazing—he gave the girls hope and told them they could earn a respectable living with their certification. They could have a house and support a family. This could be their beginning.

Family was allowed to come. Bill couldn't get off work, but I drove down myself; we were so proud of her and I wanted her to know it! Her mom's parents were there too. They showed such tremendous support to her when she was in prison. I couldn't ask for better grandparents for her! The best part of the day was we got to sit by her; we got to touch her—like she was a real girl at a real graduation *because it was true*!

I thanked the warden and told her how much Jessi loved and respected her. She smiled and told me that her goal was to make sure they were successful and never came back. She was doing a great job!

Jessi was due to get out about six months earlier than planned because of all the extra work she had done. Her welding certification would expire before she was out, so the warden arranged for her to go back and get recertified and she passed once again!

Then we learned the coolest thing—she was being featured on the cover of a magazine! She was beautiful (she is always beautiful)! There she was full cover with her welder in her hands. I may only be her stepmom, but I couldn't have been more proud if she had come from my womb. That's my girl, and the best part is, she was proud of herself.

In prison, she sopped up all the Jesus stuff she could. Her faith was really strong and she knew He was bringing her through it; she couldn't have done it on her own. The prison also gave her other class opportunities so she could think about what-if situations and how she would respond before she was in a real situation where she could slip back into old habits. They were preparing her to succeed outside the walls where she was protected from a lot of the outside pressures.

She told us, if she wanted to get high in prison, she could. The drugs were there, but the reward for staying clean was too great and she wanted a new life.

Finally, the day came when she could get out! They gave her a contact that would help her secure a job in Indiana closer to Michigan so she wouldn't be five hours away. She went to the interview and landed the job. They loved her (and how could they not, she is really awesome!). But we had a problem—no one rents places to live to felons.

Her darling grandpa had the car we gave Jessi when she worked at McDonald's. He replaced the motor and got it going and he said he'd give it back to her, but in the meantime, he drove to Indiana to take her to interviews or anywhere she'd need to go. He went so above and beyond for her, but he loved her and he was going to do anything and everything to help her win.

She started her job and her mom paid for her to stay in a hotel, but we were getting desperate.

Finally, I told Bill, "We need to find a house and buy it. She can rent from us. Worse case, we can sell it. Best case, she can live in a house, not an apartment, and eventually it will be hers and it will be a lot nicer for less money." He agreed.

We told Jessi what we were thinking and she was blown away. We went to look at five houses, I think. The one that was all redone was the smallest and the cheapest, but it was cute cute cute! But then Jessi said, "I don't want it."

What? How could she not want it?

She said, "I don't know that I want to live there for thirty years. What if I have a family and want something bigger?"

I asked her, "Why do you think you need to live there for thirty years?"

She replied, "Because aren't mortgages thirty years?"

Oh my word—I had never thought about the reality that Jessi was thirty years old and had never learned the things adults know. She had been a roamer for thirteen years. I told her, "Jessi, the loan is for thirty years, but we could sell the house in four months—and then the money we get for the house just pays off the mortgage."

"Oooh! I thought I had to live there the whole time! Then, yes, yes, yes! I want the little house!"

So Jessi moved into her little house. Her mom and I helped her with the furniture. She got housewarming gifts from other family members, and everyone was over the moon for her.

She got promoted at work within months of starting and has already had a few raises. She has a 401(k) that she plans to have be worth a million dollars when she retires (I told her that is possible and that thrills her). She pays me from every check for her house. She says she is adulting for the first time in her thirty years! I could not be more proud.

She reminds me she is an addict and always will be one. I know that. The little voice in my head still worries (because I do multitask and I can pray and worry at the same time) that I will one day lose her from this earth, but I know this for 100 percent certainty, no one can pluck her from His hand. If drugs win her life here, she has a life in Heaven and I have no doubt she is going there one day when she dies. I hope it's when she is eighty-plus years old. If it is sooner, God has prepared my heart all these years for that possibility. I cannot love her more and she knows it. I am one proud s'momma of my wonderful girl!

CHAPTER 20

God Deposits Special People Who Give Us Priceless Lessons

Debbie

When I was going to the Lutheran church when I was married to Robert, I started teaching a developmentally disabled Sunday school class. I loved those ladies so much!

Some of them were nonverbal. Others could speak, but I had to spend a while with them before I truly could understand them without having to concentrate and ask "What?" way too many times to make me comfortable.

One of the ladies, Deb, especially touched my heart. She had a special gift—she could remember everyone's birthday. She asked, "When is your birfthday?" and then it was forever in her brain. As the day approached, she would say, "Your birfday is coming up, Diane, September first. And Abbie's is October 17—hers is right after mine. Mine is October 9, Diane. Don't you forget—I'll remind you!" and she would!

Deb liked lasagna and she would tell me that often—just like she would remind me of her birthday. She would tell me, "Diane, I like lagsanya. You can have us over for dinner and you can make it for us." Us being the ladies that lived with her in her adult foster care home run by a very kind lady named Wanda.

I took her out to dinner for lasagna a couple of times, but she wanted to come to my house—they all wanted to come to my house for "lagsanya." At the time, I was living in a small house on my own—it was after Robert and I were divorced and it was just about a block from Wanda and the ladies' home. So we set a date.

Even though it was a block away, I picked them up in my car because it was winter and it was very cold. The ladies got out of my car and traipsed into my little house, cast aside their coats, and sat at the table waiting for the lagsanya to be done.

Not too long after they were there, I realized it was cold inside. I looked at the thermostat and it was in the fifties. I was out of fuel oil. It was uncomfortable. I asked them, "Do you want to go home? I can't fix the temperature until tomorrow. We can do this another time."

They all looked at me, and Deb, the verbal representative of the group, said, "No, we'll stay. We'll just wear our coats." And they did.

As all of us in our coats waited for the lagsanya, I noticed one of the nonverbal ladies pick up a small calculator that was sitting on my counter. She was punching the buttons. I didn't mind—it didn't work anymore and I needed to get a new one.

She brought it to me and held it out. I told her, "I know—the numbers don't light up anymore. It's broken. I need to get a new one. I'm sorry."

She didn't say anything because she couldn't, so she just went and sat down at the table. Then, she noticed a coffee cup filled with pens on the counter as well. In the cup, there was a small screwdriver in the midst of the pens. I watched her go to the cup and retrieve the screwdriver. Then, she proceeded to remove all the little tiny screws that were holding the top and bottom of the calculator together.

I smiled. I didn't care—it didn't work anyway. It was cold and her stubby fingers still managed to turn the screwdriver into the tiny ends. Who taught her to do that? I wondered.

A few minutes later, she had the back off the calculator, messed around inside, and proceeded to put it back together. Then she tapped the keys on the front and seemed satisfied with what she had done—she handed me the little calculator. I couldn't believe it; she fixed it!

I was stunned. I looked at her and she just looked the other way—checking out other things in my kitchen like it was no big deal. But it was a big deal to me. She was amazing! I guess Deb had a gift of remembering birthdays, and she had a gift for fixing small electronics. Wow!

Some years later, Wanda, who was old when I met her, was unable to care for the ladies anymore. Deb had a stroke and was moved to a nursing home across town. It broke my heart. I never thought about what happens to these people who can't live on their own and then their caregivers can no longer be caregivers.

I went to see Deb in the nursing home. She would matter-of-factly tell me why she didn't live with Wanda anymore and that she'd had a stroke and had to live here now. I was sad, but she seemed okay—except that she looked sad because one side of her mouth drooped a little now making it slightly more difficult to understand her, but we had been friends for so many years that I could comprehend her just fine.

She looked at me and said, "Diane, can I tew you sumpfin?"

I said, "Sure, Deb," and I smiled because she warms my heart like no other.

She proceeded to recite to me John 3:16. But when she was done, she kept reciting through verses 17, 18, 19, 20, and 21. I started crying softly. How could she do that? Who had taught her all the verses? I don't know of a "normal" friend who knows all the verses and can recite them with such beauty as she could.

She looked at me and sadly said, "I sorry, Diane. I didn't mean to make you cwy. Why did I make you sad?"

I told her, "Oh, Deb, you don't make me sad. You make me happier than anyone else ever can. I'm so glad God gave you to me as my friend because I love you."

She said, "I wuv you too, Diane. You can go now. I wiww see you later. Bye, bye."

Visits with Deb never last more than five minutes. But they are five minutes that mean the world to her…and mean the universe to me.

Heaven holds so much promise for me—I can't wait. For God tells us what heaven will be like and there will be no brokenness. We will be perfect. To me, Deb is perfect in ways that others can never be. She could never imagine saying, or I'm sure even thinking, an unkind word. She is more beautiful and true than many of my other friends. I can't wait to see her whole, and one day, I know I will because Deb most certainly loves Jesus! On June 30, 2020, God took my dear Deb home to be with Him. Goodbye for only for now, my friend.

Chris

When I was in school, I never really understood that kids were different from me. I know I was and am still naïve, but I was brutally shy until I was twenty-one when God released my crazy. I thought people who didn't talk much were just shy like me.

One boy, Chris, was especially shy. He was never in my classes, but I knew who he was and I would pass him in the hall between classes. Because I knew how hard it was being shy, when I saw him looking at the floor, I made an extra effort to say, "Hi, Chris!"

He would reward my hi by looking up sideways out of the corner of his eye, still keeping his face toward the floor, and he would smile and say, "Hi," and off he would go.

I never had any other contact with Chris during school except our short exchanges in the hall until my thirtieth class reunion. Chris was there! Only he had changed *a lot*!

He had grown at least a foot and was now a man and he no longer was staring at the floor.

I was so happy to see him. I went over to him and smiled and said, "Chris, you have grown huge!"

His return smile was beaming. He said, "I know! I have!"

It was then I realized Chris had developmental disabilities. He had been shy, but there was more to his "differentness" than I had understood until that moment. It made me love him even more.

He was so joyful to see me. He said, "Diane, I want to thank you for being my best friend in school. Can I take a picture with you?"

He not only made my day but he made my century! "Sure!"

So he pulled his wind-up disposable camera from his pocket, wound it, and proceeded to empty the camera with pictures of the two of us. He talked to me a lot—neither one of us shy with each other anymore. He told me he lived in a condo and he had a job. Seeing him was the best present I got at our reunion!

I saw him a month later at the county fair. He picked me up and sat me on his lap and hugged me like he would a treasured puppy. He told me, "Diane, you are my best friend." I suppressed my discomfort of having a big guy hold me like that because I knew he meant nothing inappropriate—he was just loving me the only way he knew how.

Every year I get a Christmas card from him and of course, it is my favorite one. Bill always smiles when he hands me the envelope and says, "Your friend sent you a card!" Inside, he signs it with a note in a boy's childish handwriting and signs it, "Love, Chris."

Yep, I cry and I thank God for giving me best friends that I will forever cherish in my heart!

Wheezie and Romer

When I decided to be a youth leader at church, I made it clear that there was no expectation of Bill to join me in leadership, but the more fun I had, the more he was willing to be involved.

Because we were a small country church, I wanted the kids to be involved in raising money for their activities during the year. Some parents didn't have the money to pay for everything we planned, so fundraising was a necessity.

We had two big fundraisers each year—a Valentine's dinner and a Flakey Bakey sale.

The bake sale was no normal sale. I had devised this Flakey Bakey sale when I was in my twenties at my old church. Church members, but especially the youth, were encouraged to make items (mostly food, but not necessarily), that would be auctioned off. That's a normal bake sale, but what made it flakey was I encouraged people to dress up flakey—aka weird! Anything but naked goes.

Since this was new to our church, I told Bill we needed to do an announcement to let people know about the sale. I said, "I'm going to be Wheezie Sludgebucket and you'll be Romer. You'll need clothes—really bad clothes because these are not normal people. We'll need to go to Goodwill."

Yeah, he wasn't too sure about this, but he went to the outlet store with me. I tried not to act too stunned that he wasn't pitching a fit. We got to the store and he picked out some rather ugly clothes. I told him, "Well, I think you need to try them on. We wouldn't want to pay for them and then find out they don't fit."

He told me, "They're fine. They'll fit. Let's go."

"No, I think you need to try them on. It will just take a minute."

He reluctantly headed to the dressing room. Now, let me explain, this is a small store. There is only one dressing room. He tried them on and shouted over the wall, "They fit!"

I told him, "Come out, I want to make sure it's the look I want."

He was not happy with me because I think he had started to change back to his regular clothes again, so I can hear some frustrated grunts coming from the other side of the door.

What I did not tell him is that there were two very beautiful young ladies waiting for the fitting room that were standing right outside his little changing space. He threw open the door and stepped out in his very ugly outfit. He looked at me full of disgust and frustration and then noticed the lovelies who were looking him up and down while smiling as they uttered, "Niiice!"

I started giggling uncontrollably as he says to me under his breath, "I hate you!"

The girls lost it as did I, but he had his outfit!

We alerted the worship leader that on Sunday we needed to do an announcement. We stayed outside the back of the church in our horrible outfits. Wheezie had a black unruly wig with a big white bow and a really bad makeup job—lipstick gone wild. She wore a polyester green and white dress with brown paisley tights underneath and some wretched flowery tennis shoes.

Wheezie came in the back of the church and up the aisle chattering away to Romer who was nowhere to be found. When she got to the front of the sanctuary, she turned around only to find that Romer was not behind her. She screamed, "Romer! Romer! Where is you, Romer?"

The door at the rear of the church opened and in came Romer pulling a very rusty wagon yelling, "Here I am, Wheezie!"

Wheezie asks him, "Romer, where you been?"

He replies, "Well, Wheezie, you said we wuz going collecting cans after church to raise money for the Flakey Bakey sale. Before church, I saw this lady chugging a beer in her car. When she was done with it, she tossed the can in her back seat and came inside. So I grabbed the can and the others she had in her backseat and I got 'em here in my wagon!"

Wheezie said, "Romer, You can't do that! It's stealing! You can't steal from the church people! You need ta give 'em back!"

Sheepishly, Romer goes over to one of the ladies in the church who is absolutely against drinking alcoholic beverages and he hands her a bag full of cans. He apologizes profusely, "I'm sorry, ma'am. Here are your cans back. I shun't have stoled them from you."

Horrified, the lady replies, "Those are not my cans!"

Romer says, "Well, yes, they are. I saw you chugging the beer before church."

She stares at him not sure what to do.

Romer stares at Wheezie.

Wheezie gives him a look like, "You better give them back now!"

Romer says to the lady, "I'm sorry, lady. You just gotta take them. Wheezie, she gets mean at me when I don't do what I'm told."

Alarmed, the lady takes the cans, says, "Fine!" and shoves them under her seat just to try to make the whole scene end.

By this time, the church is hysterical with laughter. Wheezie and Romer move to the front of the church and fill people in on the details of the bake sale.

The night of the event, our little church raised thousands of dollars from baked goods and the Flakey Bakey sale is born and becomes a crazy highlight of the church year.

Who says Christians don't have fun?

Now, the interesting thing was, the lady we picked on had out-of-town family with her in church that day. We had no idea! Oops! Of course, her brother, who was the out-of-town guest, thought it was the coolest trick to play on his sister ever and her adult kids thought it was quite hysterical as well. The lady? She still loves me— thank you, Jesus!

A few years later, Bill told me Romer died and he wasn't going to do it anymore. People at the church thought that was sad, but I guess we'd been married long enough for him to tell me no and get away with it.

Wheezie showed up again once Abbie was in high school marching band. The band needed to raise funds for a trip to Disney to march at Magic Kingdom. I shared with the band director about the Flakey Bakey and he thought it was a fun idea.

Again, I felt it was important to give an announcement to the kids in band so they knew what was happening.

So I resurrected Wheezie's outfit and showed up at all the band classes in the middle school and high school. It was interesting signing in at the office. The ladies in the office weren't too sure about me at first. I got some stares. It was marvelous.

Abbie knew I was coming to school. I asked her when lunch was in the high school because I would be there all day long, so I'd need to eat at some point (and I was not going out to lunch!). She told me the two times for lunch. I said, "I thought there were three lunch hours." She looked me in the face and said, "No, there are only two now."

So I appeared at the middle school in the morning. When I finished (and it went well—although I learned all middle school kids do not yet have a sense of humor, so many were confused about my appearance), I went to the high school and headed to the cafeteria early. I knew there wasn't any lunch at that time, but I thought perhaps I could catch the end of the lunch period prior.

When I got there, I found a table of developmentally disabled kids eating their lunch. Not thinking about my looks, I asked them, "Can I eat with you?" They replied sheepishly, but politely, "Sure," and the moved over a bit to allow me to sit down.

Not five minutes later, the cafeteria started to flood with students. It was then I realized that they let these other kids come in early so they could get their food and get seated before everyone else came through the lines.

Imagine Abbie's surprise when she started to walk by me at the table and notices Wheezie Sludgebucket eating at a table! She said, "Mother, what are you doing here?" I replied, "Imagine this—I found out there's a lunch period right now!" She was horrified and disgusted and quickly walked to find the furthest table away from me possible. Oh, the joy of being a mom!

After all the students were seated and were enjoying their conversation, the table of students next to mine started to notice old Wheezie. This was the table where the kids with piercings and unique hairstyles were sitting. Imagine them thinking I looked weird? It was beautiful!

Finally, one of them got up the courage to come over to me. She politely asked, "Um, my friends and I, we wanted to know if you are for real or are just for fun?"

I replied loudly saying, "Oh, honey, I'z jus for fun! My husband would poke his eyes out with needles if I was for real!"

She laughed hysterically and ran back to the table and said, "She's just for fun!" Then they came swarming over and asked if they could take pictures with me. I guess what's funny when you're someone else's mom is quite different than when it's your own mom!

A mom's job is never done! Haaa! PS—we raised a lot of money for the band and the Flakey Bakey carried on for a number of years. A good time was had by all (even Abbie!)

Shark Girl

Despite Bill's statement that he never wanted to hang out with those freaks from church, eventually he would tell me, "You know, Pastor Pat is probably the best friend I'll ever have."

I replied, "You mean the king of the freaks?"

He rolled his eyes and said, "I never had Christian friends before. They really care—their friendship is true."

Yes, absolutely!

When Pastor Pat and his wife, Colleen, and their five kids moved from Kansas to Country Christian Evangelical Free Church in Michigan, we had no idea how deeply we would fall in love with them, but as Lake Superior, is the deepest freshwater lake in the world, so deeply runs our feelings for them.

Katie Rose was once little, but as with every kid, she got big—she is as tall as her dad! She still retained her little girl cute face. She's one of those people who smiles with her whole face and just makes the world happy as she radiates love from every cell!

Even though I was one of those people, like my dad, who's allergic to kids, we're like mouse bait and seem to attract them, too. The Clarey kids were no exception—especially Katie and that was so okay with me. The fact that I am thirty-five years older than her doesn't seem to be a factor. Slumber parties were still something we enjoyed together. Katie would bring her sister or other girlfriends from church. Once, they even convinced Bill to let them paint his toenails telling him he needed to wear sandals to church. First, his toes are huge and why they would even want to paint them is beyond comprehension, but they did and he did, but there was no sandal wearing on Sunday (although if they'd have pinned him down and removed his shoes and socks, the proof was still evident). Oh my, I wonder what the elders would have thought about such a travesty! But the girls were hysterical doing the deed, and when it came to the Clarey kids, neither one of us would ever say no!

One summer, we were having a girls' retreat at the house that Bill built. He was working across the lake at a friend's house putting in a sea wall and I was taking the girls tubing with the speed boat.

It was Katie's turn. She had a couple of trips around the lake, and it was time for her to come in so we could switch tubers. She was in the water holding on to the tube. I put the boat in neutral, she grabbed the tube, and we pulled her toward the boat. There was a tiny ladder at the back of the boat to the right of the motor that led to the platform where they could climb on and finish their ascent into the boat. We got Katie to the edge of the boat, and as she started to get to the ladder, she screamed, "Ouch! I think the motor cut me!"

I freaked out. I went to the controls and the shifter was in the neutral position, but it wasn't locked in—I pushed the lever just one-fourth inch further and heard the thud of it switching gears from drive into neutral. The motor had been moving!

I ran to the back of the boat and Katie said, "I'm okay. Just throw me a towel. I will wrap my leg. I don't want to look at it."

She said and I obeyed. She swam closer to the boat again and somehow managed to climb up the ladder and onto the boat without losing the towel.

I sped as fast as possible across the lake to where Bill was working. I yelled to him, "Go get the car and take it to the dock! Now!"

He said, "No, I am busy."

I screamed, "I cut Katie's leg with the prop! I need to take her to the hospital—now!"

Bill dropped everything and said not another word. He turned and ran.

By the time I had reached the other side of the lake, which wasn't that far, Bill had driven around the lake in his truck, gone to our house, retrieved my car, and was parked at the dock. I later asked him, "How did you do that? How fast were you driving?"

He said, "Fast—really, really fast!"

Katie sat in the back seat of the car so she could prop her leg up on the console between the bucket seats. Her mom should have been so proud—she knew to prop her leg up to slow the blood flow and she was applying pressure to her leg. Katie was so calm.

We got to the hospital and I ran inside. They brought out a wheelchair and whisked her inside and put her on a bed. The doctor removed the towel and it was the first time I was able to see her leg. The cut was all along her shin—it was at least eight inches long and in the middle was probably cut three inches wide. God, I fileted her leg wide open!

Katie laid there with no tears. Her friend had seen her leg but was being strong for Katie. There was no blood *anywhere—not even on the towel!*

We had to call Pastor and Colleen so we could get permission to treat her and so I could tell them that I had tried to kill their daughter.

Katie told her mom, "Yeah, Mom. I'm fine. No, you don't need to come. They'll just stitch me back up and I'll go back to Diane's. We're going to have ice cream."

She is laying there cut open wide enough to put a chicken leg in the gash and she's telling her mom she's fine.

Colleen asked to speak to me. I could tell she was afraid, but she was trying to be strong and asked me, "Is she really all right? Should I come?"

I told her she seemed fine and we'd probably be okay. Colleen gave consent to treat and let me just stay with her—me the slicer lady!

She had about thirty billion stitches and still no blood. Katie later admitted it hurt really bad, but she wanted that ice cream! The doctor said it was the one place on her body that she could be sliced open and not bleed as there are not any veins or arteries right along the bone. A miracle!

We went back home and I helped Katie to the chair in the living room. She told everyone she was fine and then looked at me and said, "Now, how about that ice cream?"

I scooped it up and gave her the bowl. At this point, I'd have given her the whole half gallon. It was then that the gravity of what happened set in and I lost it. I started crying, "I hurt my Katie! I hurt my Katie!"

She said, "Come here."

I went to her and like a little mama, she hugged me and told me she was going to be just fine. When I stopped crying, she let me up and went back to her ice cream.

The guilt of hurting her was overwhelming. If only…if only… if only

I sent Katie a get-well card every day with a $1 bill inside. That was just to make her laugh because $1 doesn't buy anything, but my Grandma Van used to send us a card at the holidays with $1 inside and it would make me smile. So I needed to make her smile.

Finally, Colleen called me one day and told me the cards had to stop. Katie was fine. It was an accident. I stopped sending cards— partly because Colleen is strict and I was afraid she would punish me if I didn't listen to her. Hee hee.

Katie was fine until a little while later when she was messing around on the sofa and fell off and it split open again. It finally did heal. She still has a scar, but she said she gets to tell people she was bitten by a shark at Lake Doster. She laughs so hard—with all of her face—and knows that I die a little bit inside all over again…until she hugs me and say, "I am okay!"

Thank you, God, for letting Katie be okay, for Katie's parents who remained calm in this horrible accident and forgave me for hurting their little girl, and for Katie's sense of humor and grace.

I never drove that boat again. There was a blood smear on the back of the boat. I wouldn't even touch the boat to wipe it off. I think it was still there when we sold it. We bought a different boat the next year, and Katie wanted to know when she could come back tubing. I think she did. This time, no sharks.

This summer, we are planning a girl's trip to the cabin up north. She's in college now, but I'm still not too old to be her friend and I am so thankful! Yes, it takes a village to raise a child and I know I'm one of her village, but it also takes just one wacky old lady to almost kill one off. I'm so thankful that God's angels were protecting her and me that day!

Jody

My friend, Nancy, who I have known since I was a teenager, told me, "You have to meet my friend. I think you two will be best friends."

Nancy is known to control my life in the best way possible. She arranges for us to do things together—she is like the lady who was the cruise director on *The Love Boat* (which if you are younger than fifty-something won't mean anything to you, but when there were only three channels on TV, this was a popular show).

When Nancy retired, her husband, Chuck, told us he was taking her away for the summer on a trip. We told Nancy we would have fun that summer without her while she was off seeing Canada and all things wonderful. Nancy came home and we hadn't done anything. If she doesn't plan it, we have no life!

I met Jody and knew Nancy was right—she was going to be my bestie! She is so joyful and fun. She is generous and kind. She says she is shy, which I can't imagine because she bubbles over like the most incredible champagne. What is super cool is Jody and her husband are certified divers, like Bill and I.

I did snorkel. After the incident with Robert on our honeymoon, it was questionable whether I would try it again, but I did on a clear day and the fish were amazing! But snorkeling cannot compare with diving! Being at the level of the living creatures in the ocean is incredible. Seeing God's amazing, beautiful creatures under the sea is beyond imagination! If heaven is more incredible than earth, I cannot fathom it, because after I came up from my first dive, I told Bill, "If I die tomorrow, my life is complete!" It was that good!

After a number of years of having Jody, and her husband, Rick, as friends, we went to Bonaire diving. The reefs there are about thirty-five yards off shore, so we literally could strap a tank on our back and walk in. They are amazing! Bonaire isn't a super popular Caribbean destination except to divers, and I hope it stays that way because it is truly my favorite place on earth (so far anyway).

Someone once said, "Don't tell God you won't do something or He'll make you do it." Over and over I say, "God, don't think I'm going to be a missionary in Bonaire!"

He's not that dumb to take the bait—He hasn't sent me to work there yet, but oh my—what a dream that would be!

There is one particular dive site where we put all of our gear on and jump from the rocks into the ocean from a cliff. Jody and I were going to do it together. I'm not sure where the guys were, but when it was time to jump, a guy that was on shore, helped us put our tanks on and stand up to take the leap. Jody is tiny and the weight of the full tank and all of our gear is heavy. We appreciated the stranger's help.

It looks like it is fifty feet above the surface, but when we look back, it isn't that far—perhaps twelve to fifteen feet, but still!

As we swam around, we saw glorious fish and coral as is typical around the island. We turned around and headed back and saw something I've never seen before—a huge school of smaller silver fish. Huge—these four letters cannot begin to scribe the thousands and thousands of fish that were in front of us. As we hung suspended, we watched as a barracuda swam into the school. He was looking for dinner and watching the whole feeding process was incredible! As he entered the school, they parted as one. How did they know where to go? As the fish entered one side, the entire school moved. Amazing. It was as if the hunter had an invisible force field around him, and as he swam forward, the gap around him stayed constant.

Sometimes he would dart forward more quickly, but the whole thing happened again—just faster.

It was unbelievable—incredible—beautiful—amazing!

We swam into the school and soon were enveloped by the school all around us. We were surrounded by silver!

We couldn't stay down forever because, of course, we don't have gills. After we climbed the ladder up and out of the ocean to the surface, we removed our regulator and screamed! Never have I seen something so amazing and to share it with my friend, Jody, was a gift.

Last year, Jody went with us to Nuevo Vallarta, Mexico. We decided to dive in the Pacific Ocean. It's much colder than the Caribbean, but ocean is ocean, so we were all about it! We had to wear wet suits because the water temperature is so much colder—we had been spoiled in Bonaire!

We took a boat out this time—no diving from shore there. We were the only two female divers on the boat, which was no big deal. The boat took us to a decent-sized rock outcropping quite a distance from shore. We would follow a dive master because the visibility was low and there was a lot of current—very different surroundings for us.

It was beautiful! The rocks were craggy and sharp and there were some sea lions basking in the sunlight on top of them. We watched one climb from the water high up to the rocky top. I don't know how he could do it without hands. It would seem that the pointy rocks would hurt his beautiful underside, but he made it—defying gravity, it seemed.

They told us the sea lions are afraid of us, but if only they weren't! Oh my goodness, it was amazing to watch them from afar! God, You had such creativity when You made Your creatures!

Once we plunged off the boat into the water, I realized I could only see a few feet in front of me and it was intimidating. I had to kick hard to keep up with the dive master. He was descending quickly, which is a problem because I have difficulty equalizing pressure in my ears and I typically go down very slowly compared to everyone else. Normally, I can see Jody and Bill beneath me and I always tell them not to worry—I will keep them in my line of sight and eventually, I will be beside them. This time, I didn't have the luxury of a slow descent; I would lose the dive master and Jody in the murky water. I pushed through equalizing by plugging my nose and pushing the air against my fingers and descended quickly. I was doing okay, but it added a little to my fear.

Jody always chuckled at me because normally, I hover over one piece of coral for a long time. I find the most amazing little things because for me, it's not about how far I go, but what I see. She bought us tank knockers—a rubber tube that goes around the bottom of a tank like a belt that has a hard ball on it. Underwater, since we can't talk, we can snap the hard plastic ball against the tank and it sends out a sound that we can hear to get each other's attention. Then we can show each other the underwater treasures we find.

I normally find lots of things. But not today; this trip, I was just keeping up so I didn't get lost.

We passed through a few layers of cold water—I'd never experienced thermal changes in water like that. It was kind of cool—literally.

There wasn't the amount of soft coral I was used to seeing in the warmer temperatures. I was honestly looking forward to the end of the dive when in front of me swam one of the sea lions. He was so close. He was like a torpedo swimming upward spinning around and around in front of our faces.

Then there was another and then another. They were zooming past us and around us.

Finally, the dive master stopped and allowed us to watch them for a while—not nearly long enough. Eventually, we moved away and went back to the boat.

When we got on board, Jody and I were clapping our hands like seals in a circus—we were so excited. Then one of the men said,

DIANE BARTON

"That was absolutely the scariest thing ever! I have been on over four hundred dives out here and not once have they come off the rocks to swim and never that close. They could have really hurt us!"

Hurt us? Oh? They could hurt us? It was the most amazing thing ever! I don't think the thought of them hurting us ever crossed our minds! They told us they could have ripped off our regulators with their flippers or rammed us. They weigh hundreds of pounds.

Nope, sorry, not believing it! I think God sent us those sea lions because He knew Jody and I would love them. Oh my, I am giddy thinking about it even now. Those sissy boys! We weren't afraid of any few hundred pound sea lions! Incredible!

God once again gave me the desires of my heart, and He did it with my friend Jody as a witness yet again. We sure see the most amazing things.

I wonder…when we get to heaven, will we be able to swim in the ocean without Jacque Cousteau's scuba equipment? Will I be like a mermaid? I sure hope so. I believe anything is possible and I think it will be most incredible, and this earth is only a foretaste of what is to come.

I know heaven is no longer something I dread like I did when I was a little girl in the Lutheran church. Oh God, bring it on! And I would love to ask if you will also bring my friend, Jody! It is one of the biggest desires of my heart!

Alaska

I love to vacation. This earth God made is absolutely amazing! I truly wish I could see it all—perhaps when I am in heaven, God will bless me with the ability to scour every smidge of it.

As much as I love going on vacation, I don't love planning vacations! Bill, however, thinks the arrangement is wonderful! He truly does nothing until it's time to pack and then he folds his clothes absolutely perfectly and places them in the suitcase; he's ready to go!

I will ask him to help me fold my clothes and he looks at me as if I've sprouted a third ear and replies, "No!"

184

I get so frustrated with him! I threaten him that one day I will make him plan a vacation because it is not easy. He replied, "Well, I hope you enjoy your trip to the mailbox because if I have to plan a vacation, that's where we'll go!" Ugh! What do I say? I know what I want to do to him, but I don't want a free trip to prison!

Bill always said he wanted to go to Alaska, so finally it was on the agenda. I told him, "This is your dream vacation! I have no idea what you want to do. You need to help me with this. What do you want to do?"

He replied, "I don't know! I just want to go to Alaska."

I gave him books. I looked at interesting things to do at each of our destination cities. I'd ask him, "Do you want to do this or that?"

"Sure." "I don't know." "What do you want to do?" Ugh, again! This was supposed to be his vacation.

I told him, "The only thing I want to do is go snorkeling."

He looked at me like I'd sprouted a fourth ear and said, "I don't want to do that."

Sigh. "Okay," I said.

A couple weeks later, he said, "You know, I've been thinking about you wanting to go snorkeling. It's the only thing you want to do. It wasn't very thoughtful of me to say no. So, yes, we can go snorkeling."

I made the plans (and all the other plans for the trip) and we were off.

I was so excited about snorkeling. Everything else was wonderful too. I was enjoying this trip a lot more than I ever dreamed possible. God's creation is absolutely incredible!

Finally, the day had arrived! We took a van from the ship to the place where we would go snorkeling. A lady picked out my very thick wetsuit and told me to put it on. Sure. It was like stuffing the entire meat section from Wal-Mart into a small sausage skin. It shouldn't have been that hard—the thing was huge, but it didn't just glide on. I pulled. I smashed. I tucked. Finally—it was up and on and I could zip it. I looked like the Michelin Man!

I waddled to the van where we climbed aboard and headed to the place where we would get into the frigid water.

When we got to the water's edge, they told us that we would be cold only for an instant because the water would circulate under our suit and our body would warm the thin layer of water. The only area of exposed skin would be around our mask. I was so excited!

They handed us our fins and told us to climb into the water, sit on the natural rock ledge, and put our fins on. Then, we could lower our masks and get in the water. They would guide us around through the water and point out things of interest.

Oh wow! I was so excited! I stepped into the water—no fear here! I got to the rock ledge and sat down—well, I attempted to sit down, but my suit was so full of air that I popped up instead of sat down!

I was horizontal on the water. I was truly a marshmallow floating in a giant cup of freezing water! I was bobbing uncontrollably around. I couldn't do anything except cry to Bill for help.

He was watching me and laughing. I said, "Help me!" He replied, "No! This is way too fun!" A true pig!

Finally, the young man who worked for the joint grabbed me and pushed my hips down on the ledge. The air zoomed out of my face hole, and I slowly sank to the ledge. I glared at Bill who had no response other than to laugh hysterically. Someday God will get him—and it had better be good!

I saw sea stars of all shapes, sizes, and colors. There were amazing sea slugs and large jellyfish. It was definitely different from the waters of the Caribbean or even Hawaii—the cold waters provided no colorful coral, but the colors of the sea creatures were amazing. Beautiful!

As we were heading back, we heard one of the guides yell. In front of us were humpback whales! They were swimming along the deep channel and we could watch their magnificent backs and flukes rising and lowering in the water! Wow!

When we got back to shore, the young man, who rescued me—the marshmallow, told us that he had been working for the outfit for over three years and he had never seen whales there. But I knew why—God gives me the desires of my heart and it was a payback for being there with Bill! Thank you, Lord, you are so good to me!

Never be afraid to ask the Lord. I know He loves to bring me joy! Tell Him the desires of your heart and wait in expectation for Him to exceed your dreams and then celebrate when He does because He is most incredible!

A Necklace of Nails

The Wings Home is a home like your house or mine. It has four bedrooms, and at this home, we care dying people in their last six weeks of life. It is a charitable home—we charge nothing to the dying person or their families. It is a gift for those in our community. We exist through private donations, and as much as possible, we staff the home with volunteers.

I am one such volunteer. I am there the first Thursday of each month from 5:00 to 10:00 p.m.

Some people call us angels. Some people say they couldn't do it, but I didn't think I could either until I tried it. Now, I know that some of the most special stories I'll have in my life will come from being there.

Dad always said when you're with a person dying, you're on heaven's doorstep. I believe that's true. Sometimes the dying say they can see people who have died before them. I think it's true. Their faces are serene, and they are looking in the distance beyond where we can see. I would love to be able to follow their eyes. God willing, someday I will!

I can't imagine the world before hospice care. I remember Robert's mom telling me that her mom died of cancer. She said if she ever had cancer, she'd kill herself because the pain her mother suffered was unimaginable and horrible. But that was before there was hospice. Our role in hospice care is to keep people comfortable and make sure they are not alone when they die.

Wings of Hope Hospice provides so many benefits to both the dying and their family. When someone says, "They're going to die— they've called hospice in. It will be any day!" I want to scream, "Nooo! They should have called hospice six months or two years ago!" There is so much they do for the families to support them in the journey.

Calling them in the last few days is like you're going on vacation and you only get to go to the airport! Put that in your memory banks and don't forget it—do you hear me?

We provide care for the last six weeks of life at the Wings Home, but we don't come with one of those pop-up timers like a turkey has, so we don't know exactly when we're at that six-week mark. The nurses are pretty good at knowing the signs, but each person is different.

There was one woman who was a patient at the Wings Home who had been there for a couple of months. She was in the room at the end of the hall. We call it the Oak Room. She was still coherent and I chatted with her as I was taking care of her. When I leaned over her, she noticed my necklace and she asked me, "Did you make that?"

I was surprised and answered her, "Yes, I did." The necklace was a cross. I bent four shiny nails and then took colored wire and wrapped it around the nails securing them into a cross formation. There was a leather cord that wrapped through the nails so it could hang around my neck.

She inquired, "What's the story about them?"

I told her that I had gone on a mission trip to Mississippi, and to raise money for my trip, I had made the necklaces and sold them for $10 each.

She asked me if I had any left.

I did—I had four of them—each wrapped with a different color wire.

She said, "I'd like three of them. I have money. I can pay you."

I didn't really want to sell them. I had made them for myself, but I seriously was going to deny the request of a dying woman? Nope! I promised her I would bring them to her the next Tuesday.

The following Tuesday, I went to the Wings Home for a board meeting and when I walked in, I handed them to a volunteer and told them who they were for—she said, "Oh, she told us you were coming today. Here is your money."

I told her, "I am not taking her money. You tell her they are a gift from me. I will stop and talk to her after my meeting is complete."

The meeting went long, and I had another meeting at church that night and I had to hurry to not be late. I asked the volunteer if she would let her know I couldn't stay, but I would stop back. She promised to tell her.

When I came back, she was gone.

God, was my meeting at church more important than stopping to see her? We never know the day or the hour God will call us home, but she was at the Wings Home and she'd been there a while. I should have never just assumed she would be there later. I was so sad. I had broken my promise.

I thought of her often. For months, I carried the guilt of not visiting her. Yes, I have a guilt issues! Regret...

Six months later, she was still on my mind—I needed to let it go! It was time to volunteer at the home again. As I thought about the night ahead, I told myself to begin anew. There would be more people to love.

Tonight, there was a lady I had never met before—she was in the Maple Room—the room with the fireplace. Unlike my friend who purchased my necklaces, she was no longer coherent. She slept soundly, seemingly comfortable.

They teach us to talk to them—they say hearing is the last sense to go. So I chattered to her as I repositioned her. As I was hustling around her bed, I noticed that she had one of those monkeys that I often see little girls hook to their school backpacks—the ones with the long arms and a piece of Velcro between their paws so they can "hold" on to things. I said to her, "Do you have a monkey? It looks like it fell off the bed. Let's pull him back up here!"

I reached over to pull the monkey so it was up beside her and could watch over her. As his head appeared over the top of the mattress, what I saw amazed me. Indeed, it was her monkey and around his neck were my three cross necklaces!

Six months ago, she left, but not to die as I assumed but to go home to her earthly home. As sometimes happens with people at the home, they get better for a while. So they go home, and then if we are blessed, they come back to us later. This had happened to her.

God blessed me by giving me the desires of my heart—desires that I thought were impossible because I believed she had died. God couldn't fix my regret, yet He did—in His most incredible and kind way! What were the chances that she would still have the necklaces? I don't recall that monkey when she had been here before.

With God there are no coincidences, but on purposes—His purposes. He gave me such joy! He took my sadness and my guilt away and replaced them with amazing love—His love for me that never ends! He can do that for you, too. Trust Him!

My First Death

One would think that volunteering at a place that cares for the dying, death would be something I encountered often, but I didn't. I think it was close to eight years that I volunteered at least once a month and I had yet to have a patient die. Bill asked me, "How are you going to handle someone dying? You are so tender!"

I would tell him, "I don't know! I will tell you when it happens."

When we raised animals to take to the fair, I knew what was going to happen to them. I enjoyed them for the time I had them. I wasn't cold or cruel. I loved them, but there was quiet acceptance. I learned Mom cried ferociously when they were hauled from the fair (not by us, but by the people that took care of such things). I suppose in my mind, I thought it was kind of like that—except we are most definitely not selling the people at the Wings Home for food!

One week, I was volunteering two days in a row because they needed extra help. I had to stop by the Wings of Hope Hospice office before I went the final block to the Wings Home for my shift. Jacquie Fillmore, who I think runs the world there, told me, "Diane, I think you're going to have your first death tonight." I guess everyone knew it had never happened to me.

So, when I got to the home, I checked on our guests and the one lady who had been there for many months was definitely declining. Her daughters and friend were there as always. We had gotten to know each other in the time our guest had been here and it was definitely more solemn than the months prior. The night went on and it was quiet. At 10:00 p.m., it was time for me to go home and she was still alive; they were still holding their vigil beside her bed.

I wasn't sure what I would find the next night. I fully expected that she would have died in the night, which they often do. But, the next evening, she was still there.

I sat in the kitchen—I don't recall that we had many patients in the house that night—maybe only two. Evenings are generally quiet.

Her daughter came from her room and was talking to me. She thanked me for what I did. I told her she was welcome. She told me, "It must be hard."

I said, "It's really not. Actually, one thing that I didn't understand until I volunteered here is that we get attached to the patients—especially those like your mom who have been here for months. But, when it's time for them to die, we aren't their family. We need to remember our place and let the family have their time."

She told me she hadn't thought of that either. She smiled and went back into her mother's room.

A while later, she came out and told me, "We need you to come into her room."

I asked her, "Is everything all right?"

She said, "Yes, it's just time and you need to come."

I followed her to her mother's room and they moved aside and said, "You stand here by mom's head." It was kind of a place of honor and I was absolutely touched. I didn't say a word but joined them as we watched her take every breath.

Her breathing slowed, and when we thought she was gone, she would breathe again. And she would breathe again. This repeated over and over until it didn't. There was no next breath...we knew she really was gone. We were silent until I asked, "Can I tell you something?"

They shook their heads yes.

I said, "I've been volunteering for eight years and I've never had a patient die before. Thank you for making this so special for me. I was really afraid how I'd handle it, but you made it all okay."

At that point, they sobbed—it was so incredible that I was there for them and they were there for me. We loved each other through it.

Their mom held on a long time for them, but it was finally time for her to go and we released her and it was more peaceful than I could imagine—for all of us!

Coach

The coach at our high school was a true manly man. His physique was solid. His hair was white and his eyes were blue and his voice was the deepest of any man I've ever heard—so deep that I almost couldn't understand him.

I never had him as a teacher, but I saw him around school and he was a presence. He cared for the young men he coached and it was evident. Our team never had a losing season—they played hard for him and they won, not because he was mean because they wanted to win for him.

When Bill and I moved back to Plainwell and Abbie was in marching band, we always went to the games. One week, it was coach's ninetieth birthday and he came to the game. He rode up on a golf cart with the guy who had been the assistant coach when I was in school. Coach was still a big man, but he was definitely old. He walked slowly and the assistant coach helped him get to his seat.

When I saw him, tears ran down my face. I told Bill who he was. He said, "He must have been an amazing teacher to you."

I said, "I never had him, but I knew who he was. He's a legend. It's why the field is named after him. He cared for all his boys—for some of them, he was probably the only one who did. His daughter had cancer, and when she died, he raised those grandchildren and he made sure all his kids had a college education. He is a true man of God!"

There was a write-up in the paper after that game. At halftime, coach went into the locker room and talked to the boys—he gave them a coach pep talk. The team said they wanted to win the game for coach that night and they did.

I had pottery nights in my basement on Tuesdays. I managed to rope many of my friends into volunteering at the Wings Home—a side effect of being my friend is that I make them come to all my charity things—I mean, it's for their own good!

One night, one of my neighbors who is a volunteer told me, "Coach is at the home."

I held it together until they went home. After they left, I went up to the living room where Bill was sitting in his Archie Bunker chair watching TV. I started crying hard. He asked me, "What's wrong?"

I said, "Coach is at the home and I volunteer Thursday!"

He told me, "You are going to have to tell them that you aren't going to do it this week!"

I shrieked, "No—No! I need to care for him! I need God to make him live until Thursday! I need to give back to him for just a little of what he has given to me!"

Bill held me until my sobbing subsided. I was spent!

Thursday came, and when I got to the home, I found out God had answered my prayers and Coach was still there. Around his room were pictures of many of the teams he had coached over the years. He was alert and could talk—although his voice was still rumbly deep and I still couldn't understand him well. We managed.

I cared for him that night. I loved on that man who had loved so many, and I praised God for yet another wish come true.

The gifts I get from caring for others is beyond imagination. Betty Jo Ferry from Wings of Hope Hospice told me that people are their best when they are giving and I think it's true. We think we are being depleted, but often, it's quite the opposite; we are being filled. We are God's hands and feet on earth when we dare to use them for His purpose. We indeed are walking on holy ground.

CHAPTER 21

Follow Me

The Plans He Has for Me

I loved working. For sure, God was my Master at work, and I knew He was watching my every step. My work ethic must have been noticed because I was asked by the president if I would figure out why we were not shipping new products on time. They put me in this special job to figure out the issues.

It really was a unique position and because it didn't really belong in any one department, where I physically sat didn't really matter. Hammer, my boss from years before, was now running the Art Department and he said I could sit in an office in his area.

What I found is that there were two departments that were the real problem for on-time shipments and one of them was the art department. They were terribly backlogged.

I was approached by an amazing man who was overseeing a few departments and he told me he had a plan to change things. He shared with me that he was going to move this person to this role, and Hammer to another role. He told me everything would be just as he wanted if I would take the art department manager position.

I knew what I'd be up against—it was one of the two departments that was an issue, so I spoke the first words that came to my mind, "I'd rather puke!" Yep, not a very professional response! Um…

He looked at me and said, "You realize I am offering you an incredible promotion. Are you sure that's your final answer?"

I told him, "No, sorry, I'll take the job."

He told me he was sure I could fix things, but I knew it was such a mess!

I worked eighty hours a week trying to figure out the backlog. Fortunately, Hammer had good metrics showing what each person was producing. I learned we didn't get further behind, but they had been working mandatory overtime for a long time, and I knew they were burned out. Employees weren't accountable or responsible for the workload or due dates; they just did what they were told. It was drudgery. Morale was bad. They were good people, but there was no reward.

I got together with my managers and we planned an off-site meeting. We each took a role in a skit showing the employees what it was like when one of our salesman sold an item and promised he would have packaging art for the new product in four weeks, our standard lead time. The *Rocky* soundtrack was playing. There was a lot of energy in the room. He made the sale! He came back and told us to start art. We had a flip chart showing the timing of all of the steps required to produce the art. We recorded each step on the chart and how long it took. Four weeks came and went. We didn't have the art done. The salesman had to go back in without the art. The music stopped. It was quiet. We failed him.

The thing we showed though is that the time it took to do the job was enough. We just didn't start it in time because we had a back-log. It was possible, but the backlog had to go.

I put them all on teams and I told them I was going to assign them 25 percent more than they normally did, but we weren't going to be on mandatory overtime. If they finished the work assigned, they could go home with pay. They perked up. But there were conditions. The whole team had to finish, so they needed to help each other, and quality couldn't suffer. We were going to do this for four weeks, and if we could accomplish this, in one month, we could take our lead time from six weeks to four weeks and allow our sales team to keep their promises.

I wasn't crazy—I told my boss before I tossed out this idea. He asked me how many teams I thought would finish early. He was concerned because he didn't think it would be okay if they all left early. It made no sense because my goal was they all would finish early, but I feared he'd say we couldn't do it, so I told him, "Well, I hope one or two teams out of eight can do it." Assured I didn't think they all would finish, he told me to go ahead.

Every team finished by the end of the day Wednesday! I was so excited for them! I kept my word and they had Thursday and Friday off to enjoy. No overtime pay for the company. No burn out for the employees. They were stoked! I was ecstatic! They were capable of so much more than I thought. I was so proud of them!

Week 2 was a repeat of the first week. They all went home at the end of the day Wednesday. They were working together. Quality didn't suffer.

Week 3—they asked me to stop. I was stunned—why? They said, "We aren't eating lunch. We aren't taking breaks. We don't want people to stop to go to the bathroom."

I laughed and told them, "I didn't tell you to finish by Wednesday! That was your deal. I hoped you'd have a half a day on Friday off with pay. I didn't tell you to wear diapers!" (They weren't, really!)

They didn't let up on their pursuit of a three-day work week, and by the end of the third week, we were able to deliver our four-week lead time.

By the end of the fourth week, we dropped our lead time from six weeks to three weeks.

A few months later, we had a slower week and reduced our lead times to two weeks. Sales was thrilled! I asked them if they wanted us to lower the lead time even more or if they wanted the ability to call when they had hot requests and we would prioritize. They chose the latter, and they now had the ability to ask for whatever they needed and we proudly delivered. We did what they requested "first, not fast" so quality need not suffer.

These most wonderful people took our quality and service from 45 to 96 percent. Turnover stopped. Morale soared. As people left, we did not backfill positions because employees were so much more productive. It took time, but I was blessed; they were the best ever! One of our salesman told me, "If the rest of the company provided service like your department, we would own all of the business!" Very nice!

Sever Me, Please!

I loved my job. I loved the people I worked with. I hated getting up in the morning, but never because I didn't like where I was going; it was because I don't like to wake up!

But I felt God telling me to leave. I had managed the art department for over twenty years. I wanted to work for Him.

I wondered if I should go work for Compassion? I certainly loved the organization and releasing children from poverty in Jesus's name is amazing and I if I could live that miracle every day—how incredible! But I was supporting fifty children—how would I manage? I never want to stop sponsoring them!

My company was selling off one of our divisions. When we did that, we would eliminate positions. My previous boss was in charge of the separation process. He was an amazing Christian man, so I asked if I could talk to him. Through tears, I explained about my fifty children and I told him I felt God was asking me to leave, but I wouldn't stop sponsoring the kids. However, if he let me go, I would get severance pay and I could use that money to pay in full my child sponsorships and I could afford to get a job with Compassion paying 60 percent less than what I was currently earning.

He looked at me with such kindness and understanding and told me, "Diane, I understand when God calls you, it's a powerful thing. Are you sure you want me to do this because I think I can make it happen."

I told him yes and he told me I should tell my current boss— the news should come from me.

I had a conversation with my boss—same tears, same story. He was supportive and told me he would miss me, but he wouldn't stand in my way. *My* plan was in motion.

But as my previous boss worked through the process to eliminate my job and sever me, human resources told him no; they wouldn't let me go.

At the time he was working through things on his end, I applied for jobs at Compassion. Silence. I received one call back, but they reluctantly admitted to me that they had called me in error; they had meant to call another applicant—their apologies.

I felt strongly my answer from God was "No."

My mom said, "Diane, maybe God just wanted to know you were willing to leave it all if He needed you." Perhaps. Relief and yet, a big disappointment. I was so willing.

As soon as I heard both doors close, my enthusiasm for my current job was almost stronger than it ever was before. I felt like I was meant to be here and I jumped back in excited to have an answer and know I was where God wanted me to be.

Retirements

About two years later, my company offered early retirement to anyone age fifty and older. They hoped 25 percent of those eligible would take it; 40 percent did. Most of our amazing leadership took it and left—including my boss and my previous boss.

I was eligible—I was fifty-three, but according to my calculations, I couldn't afford it. I would stay until I was sixty—then I would get my retention stock; I would be financially okay. I had it all planned out.

When much of our leadership retired, it was scary for some areas. I'll admit I was nervous, but when people told me negative things about my new leadership, I'd say, "I'm going to remain optimistic and until I see it with my own eyes, I'm going to choose to have an open mind."

One of my first bosses said, "Oh, Di, I am very concerned for you. You have always been the person who will stand up and speak for what is right. It's why everyone respects you. One day, you will speak up and she [my new leader] won't like it and she'll get rid of you."

I told her I had been warned, but I was just going to do my best and try not to worry about it. I knew I would be true to God, myself, and my employees. I didn't want to live afraid. But I'll admit, I was a dog in a cage now. I had to ask permission for my every move from someone who didn't know my job as well as I did, and I felt like my cage was too small and it was cutting into my skin. Just five and a half more years and I could retire.

That summer, I attended Ladies' Day at Gull Lake Ministries where I heard Rebekah Lyons speak. I felt like there was no one else in the room except Rebekah and me. She said, "If God tells you to jump, jump. Don't look for the net—just trust Him and do it." That day, I knew God was talking through her to my heart. I knew I needed to quit my job.

Then I got home and looked for the net. I got scared.

I told my mom, "God is going to have to boot me if he wants me to leave. I love my job and my staff too much to go." I disobeyed God again.

In February, I was given my annual performance review. It was outstanding. I was rated above standard in code of conduct. My boss told me, "Rating someone exceeds in this area is unheard of, but you speak up when things aren't right. You are an example to follow around the company." That felt good; I believed she trusted me to speak honestly.

I had told my boss we needed some software solutions. I shared with her what would work and how it would help not only my department but four other departments. We could eliminate chance of error while improving speed and productivity. We were pretty excited.

After the presentation to my boss, I was told to wait. For one and a half years, I was told to wait. I could have implemented the technology in the time I was waiting, but I no longer had the authority to work with other departments and get things done. There was a chain of command now.

The company hired a director of eCommerce, and I was so excited to have him here—someone who knew what they were doing. With this new eCommerce leader, I had hope we would get what we needed.

There was a team who decided what new solution we would pursue, but I did my homework because I knew what I was seeing was fraught with issues. I double-checked with many contacts in the industry and asked if my concerns were valid. They said yes and helped me to understand why so I could put together a document for the team. My goal was to make sure my leadership would understand; I wanted to wipe any doubt from their minds so they could make correct decisions.

When I presented my concerns and with supporting information I had learned from contacts in industry, I was chastised.

In April, I was written up for my code of conduct—for not being a team player. For being manipulative. I was destroyed. The things that were said in my write-up were inaccurate. I was the example to my employees about learning from mistakes—I made a lot of them over the years and owned them, but this was new—being blamed for trying to do the right thing; I didn't know how to handle it. I was so hurt.

I tried to explain the concerns to my boss. I don't know if she understood or not, but I tried to be patient. I tried to teach her. My employees did the same when she talked to them. Finally we met with the new company who was supposed to provide the solution, and they confirmed they could not do the things I thought were an issue, but my boss did not understand.

The same day, my boss came to my office. She told me I should just stay home and babysit my grandchildren. She asked me what other jobs I wanted; she didn't want to just give me a severance package if there was something else I wanted to do. I told her I was doing what I loved. She shook her head no.

I met with human resources. I told him about the conversation with my boss. He was stunned. He said he would have a meeting with the three of us. He never did.

I asked another human resource manager for an investigation of my write-up. She said she would do it. She never did.

I was left with a choice. Continue to be persistent trying to teach my boss that the company was going to spend a half a million dollars on a solution that wouldn't work, or I could lie and say it would work when she asked. I couldn't lie.

Every time my boss asked me if it would work, I would politely explain why it did not function as required. Every time she took notes and it seemed like she was trying to understand, but it didn't feel right.

I told my employees I knew I would be let go. They begged me to just let it fail; they would rather not even use computers if it meant losing me as their boss.

I didn't bring the subject up to my boss anymore, but when she would ask me, I respectfully told the truth. God sees my every move. I had to be truthful. She never told me she was upset with me or I wasn't performing, but there were signs. She started meeting one on one with my employees without me. She started filtering my email. None of these things were normal.

In August, I was given a choice—I could be on a performance improvement plan because of my poor performance or I was offered the opportunity to leave. Finally, I jumped and trusted God to provide the net. The human resources person told me, "Diane, I am going to tell you something that will hurt you, but you need to know. People don't like you. You are difficult to get along with." Slap!

We have a policy that says if an employee raises up concerns, there cannot be retaliation. Everything I knew about this company I loved was coming unraveled. It was time for me to go.

As word got out that day and the months that followed, people called me sobbing, yelling, and swearing. People were angry and sad. I did my best to calm their fears while my own were raging. I was showered with love—that human resources lady was wrong. She did not know me at all, but she believed what she had been told.

I had a choice to be angry or understand that God had asked me to jump the year before and I told mom He'd have to boot me and He did. If I didn't listen, He would get my attention and He did.

One summer, my mom and I went to a women's retreat. They had a zip line and it looked really fun. My mom was probably about seventy, but no matter her age, she is spicy and never wants to sit on the sideline—my grandma was that way, so I guess it's in her genes! When we stood looking at the zip line, Mom said, "I want to do that!"

So we got in line, and when we got to the top, I had her go in front of me. The young man helped her into the harness and connected it to the zip line. She's small—and standing there, I thought about how little she really was. The thought of jumping scared her— it was a long way down. Jump—with no net. She looked at the young man and asked, 'Can I sit down?"

He replied, "Sure" and he helped her sit.

Perched on the edge of the very tall structure, she scooched her tush forward—well, she really never moved, but her upper body pretended to scooch forward. She asked him, "Can you push me?"

He said, "No, ma'am, we're not allowed to push people off the platform."

Mom did her pathetic little scooching while not-scooching thing. The line behind her was getting longer and longer. We didn't have three cycles of the moon to wait on little mom. Finally, the guy looked around and shoved Mom from the ramp.

After a split second, I could hear Mom scream, "Wheee!"

I came down behind her and she said, "Wasn't that just the greatest? You know, he pushed me!"

I laughed; yes, he pushed her and she loved it.

God pushed me from my job because I wouldn't jump. I didn't love the push. I hoped I eventually would find the "Wheee," but right now, I just hurt.

People asked me what I was going to do. I didn't know. I was lost. I spent a huge amount of day answering phone calls assuring everyone I was okay even when I wasn't feeling that way.

My retired neighbor, Karen, asked me how I was and I told her, "Lost."

She asked me if I was a list person. I told her, "I was, but not now."

She said, "Make a list. You need to know you're doing something."

I did and that helped. I finished things on our house—things that had driven me nuts for two years. I painted all the exterior doors inside and out, but with every stroke of the brush, I heard the painful words in my head, "Diane, people don't like you. Diane, you are difficult to get along with." Even though I knew it wasn't true, I still heard her words. My heart knew it wasn't true, but my head was listening to the lies, Satan's lies.

I told people that I didn't know what I was going to do; I was going to focus on my exhale and listen for God's voice. That was true and that gave me peace.

Jesus Loves Me This I Know

Feeling lost and hurt after being let go, Bill and I went to a picnic to celebrate Wings of Hope Hospice. Marcia, the lady that hosts the picnic every year, does everything so beautifully—it would be a great day! I was really happy to get out and visit because they are such loving people and I was feeling rather broken and alone.

Nancy, the previous executive director of Wings of Hope Hospice, and some other ladies at her church make beautiful lap quilts. They have each guest that stays at the Wings Home pick one out for their family to keep as a memory of their stay. The quilts are not made with ugly scraps of polyester pantsuits; instead, they're stunning. If only I didn't have to be dying to get one!

At the picnic, Nancy had one of the beautiful quilts and she was selling tickets for it. She would use the money raised from the quilt raffle to buy more fabric. Bill bought twenty tickets and put my name on them. I thought, "God is going to give this to me because there is a beautiful heart in the middle of the quilt and he wants me to know that He loves me. I am not alone." Seriously, I just knew He would give it to me and I thought it was incredibly thoughtful of Him.

I wasn't going to tell Nancy that she could stop selling the tickets—I mean, the money was for a good cause!

The most darling little old man was the one chosen to draw the winning ticket. He was absolutely precious! He reached in, pulled out a ticket, and handed it to Nancy. She looked me in the eyes and said, "Diane Barton!"

I screamed and ran up and snatched the quilt. I had to tell Nancy the story of how I was so hurt from losing my job; how I felt so broken. I knew God had a plan and that He loved me and I felt He was saying to me, "See this heart quilt? This represents the love I have for you! You are not alone. Remember this!"

When I shared with her, she said, "Diane, yes, you needed to have that quilt. This is such an amazing story!" Indeed, it was because Jesus loves me. Jesus loves you. He is not a God that died with the Bible; He is a God that lives in the Bible and lives today and loves today. Be open to His presence, His love, His purpose. He is most incredibly wonderful! He is always with us. We are not alone. We are not forgotten. He has a plan. Every day I make my bed and I look at that quilt and I know He is with me.

My Plan

I have conducted cooking classes in my home for charity. I was worried (do you get it by now that I worry a lot?) that I wouldn't be able to take care of my Compassion kids. Hello? Had I been taking care of them? No, God had, but I was reverting to this feeling that I needed to provide instead of trusting.

So I had this great idea—I would teach cooking classes and I would use the money from the class to sponsor the kids. Great idea! I got that figured out. I actually had a class scheduled for one of the charities, and I ran *my* idea by them. They loved it! Excellent!

About two and a half months after being booted, I remember telling Bill, "I am happy. I am really happy." He gave me the biggest hug. He had been so supportive of me through all this. Prior to the "boot," he told me, "You can quit, but only if you get another job." But, after watching my anguish when I was fired, he never mentioned another job. He just supported my healing and working through it and my strong belief that God had never given up on us and I knew we would be okay because God would see to it. I was finally at peace about it.

I had joined a Bible study class and I was loving it. God was really speaking to me through the study. For a number of years, I felt God wanted me to write a book—a God book about all the miracles He has done for me in my life. But I never had time. I hoped that if I wrote the book, it would open doors for me to share about my journey and God would use it to bring people to Him. I felt the pull to do it more strongly than ever.

I could use the cooking class as income while I did my dream of living for God.

One of the Bible study lessons for the week was "No Backup Plan." Seriously!

I went to our class and I told the ladies about my idea for the cooking class. One of the women said, "That's a great idea! You should do that."

But wait—wait! This week, God said, "No backup plan." It made me realize that He was thumping me upside the head *again*— "When are you going to stop planning your life and start living the one I have for you?"

My answer that week was, "Right now!"

My dilemma is that when I'm at home, I will not stop the gotta-dos. I knew I needed to go away. Our cabin in Michigan's Upper Peninsula would be a great spot to write, but it was winter and it's a ten-and-a-half-hour drive there in the summer.

I decided to ask in my Christmas letter if anyone knew of a place where I could go to write. Literally, that week, a wonderful lady, Susan, who leads the prayer group at church, told me she needed me to stay after our time of prayer was over. She said to me, "I'm so glad you're here. I talked to Bob and we want you to stay in the upstairs apartment of our carriage house. It's only a few minutes away and it's quiet. All we ask is that you give me a signed book when you're done."

I was not surprised at God's prompt answer to prayer.

Susan took me to the carriage house and showed me around. It was perfect. She put the key to the door in my hand and I sit here now, blessed and writing just as God planned.

When He says jump, He catches me. If there is a net required, He provides it.

My only regret?—why am I such a difficult learner? Had I jumped when God told me to jump, I would not have been booted. I could have walked in His path on my own.

I can just imagine God standing in Heaven talking with two angels. They're watching me. One of the angels asks God, "Why does she do that? There is an open doorway, yet she slams into the wall right beside it." God replies to the angel, "You wouldn't believe it if I tell you." They all shake their head. Yet God doesn't give up on me.

My praise—God loves me despite my choices. When I don't believe in myself, He never gives up hope. His will be done on Earth as it is in Heaven. Amen!

What will I do? Whatever God tells me to do. I am here for Him; waiting for Him to take my Hand and lead me through the door, down the path, and into His perfect plan. I am His. Thank you, God, for never giving up, for being persistent, and for loving me despite myself.

Is God tugging at your heart? Are you feeling lost and alone? Are you feeling empty? Is there a hole in your heart? Do you have a sadness that won't go away? Let Him in. Don't be afraid. If you are stubborn like me and walk down your own path, He has to bring us back around and sometimes it hurts to be reprimanded—as adults, just like when we were disciplined as children, but with God, it is always out of love.

Revelation 3:19–20 states, "Those whom I love I rebuke and discipline. So be earnest and repent. Here I am! I stand at the door and knock. If anyone hears My voice and opens the door, I will come in and eat with him, and he with Me."

Be earnest and repent. Remember when your parents told you to apologize? With God, our perfect parent, He requires the same. He allows us to own our sin and then He takes it away—never to be mentioned again. It is gone as far as the east is from the west. We are wiped clean, forgiven, washed with His blood on the cross because *He loves us! He loves you.*

He can indeed fill the void, heal the hurt, and fill us with bless-
ings overflowing. If He is knocking, let Him in. Call out to Him;
He will complete you and complete the work He began in you and
when God does something, it will be beautiful and magnificent; just
you wait!

Dear Heavenly Father, please come to me. Lord, You know why
I hurt. You know my troubles. You know my worries. Take these burdens from me, Lord. I know I am a sinner. I am sorry for my sins and
ask You to take them from me. Give me peace and let me begin anew
walking hand in hand with You. You are my perfect partner. You will
never leave or forsake me. You are my all in all. Fill my cup, Lord. Be
my Lord and Savior. Put your arm around me, sweet Jesus and walk
with me always. I love you forever. Amen.

EPILOGUE

Christians Don't Sin When They Walk with God

Whatever! I've heard people excuse my sin for me and say things like, "Well, you must have come back to God after you sinned."

No, I was always walking with God throughout my sin. I never stopped going to church—in fact, I went more. I went to Bible study. I surrounded myself with godly people. I wanted God to take Dean away from me, but he didn't because I needed to end my sinful relationship. I needed to stop. I needed to give that relationship back to God. I chose to live every day in sin.

I still sin! I will always sin. The Bible talks about sins all the time—it wouldn't need to if we could take a magic pill and not do it. But the Bible says in Romans 3:23–24 New International Version (NIV): "For all have sinned and fall short of the glory of God, and all are justified freely by His grace through the redemption that came by Christ Jesus."

It absolutely does not say, "For all *who haven't become believers yet* have sinned." Absolutely not. We have sinned and will sin until Christ comes and takes us home to perfect heaven where there is sin no more. Only in heaven there is no sickness, there is no pain, there is no death—there is God in heaven with us and it will be beautiful!

Just like when people ask "How could God let this happen?" We let it happen when we brought sin into our lives in the garden and every day since then. We ruined His perfect plan. God can't sin! He is perfect.

He saved us. He will save us. When we live with Him in heaven, then it will not be allowed, but we are living the life we chose in the garden and we choose every day.

Do I cheat on my husband now? No and God-willing, I never will. God gave Bill to me and I am so thankful. I hope I learn from my sin and repent, and do not do that same sin again, but rest assured, I can come up with new ones. I didn't have boxes of chocolate and caramel covered ice cream bars when I was a kid, but I do now and I eat them! I do not take care of my temple like I should.

I do not control my tongue like I should.

I do not talk to God throughout the day like I should. I know He is with me, but I could be so much better!

Do I put on my armor every day like the Bible tells me? No, but I am working on it!

But, here's the bottom line, I will never be good enough. I will never stop sinning until I'm in heaven with Him. I will always need Jesus. I will always appreciate and value that to be in heaven someday despite myself, I needed Him to save me and He did!

I hung Him there on that cross and every day He dies for me. In my mind, I see Him hanging there—His beaten, bloody body hanging there telling me, "I love you more than life itself, more than the most extreme pain and sorrow you have felt in your life here on earth." I never had it as bad as Jesus did when He was beaten and hung on a cross to die—bloody beyond recognition *for me*. If I want to feel sorry for myself even one day, I can think of Him and the sacrifice He gave for me and say, "Suck it up, buttercup!" He paid it all.

I implore you to learn from my lessons—walk closer to Him. Know He is with you in the shadows of the valley of death. He never leaves you; He is right there—if only you dare to reach out your hand to touch His hand when you are in the dark and ugly places you choose to go. Instead, have faith like Peter to step out of the boat when you see Jesus and walk to Him—even on water. But, when you, like me, doubt like Peter, and we start to sink, "Reach out Your hand, oh Jesus, and pick us up in our lack of faith and save us!"

I want to evermore treasure the gifts He has given to me—even the trials because they have made me a better person, a stronger person, a person more appreciative of what He has done for me and the wonderful people He has used to surrounded me. He is my Savior and I am so blessed!

Thank You, Jesus, for saving me, a miserable sinner. Thank You for loving me every day. For being my Perfect Man. My Perfect Savior. My Perfect God Almighty!

If you have not asked Jesus to be your loving Savior and you feel Him knocking at the door of your heart, ask Him now, won't you?

"Oh Most Heavenly Father, I come to You as a sinner. I believe You came to die for my sins. You hung on that cross because You loved me and I am so grateful, Lord Jesus for Your sacrifice for me. I confess my sins to You, and ask for Your forgiveness. I ask You to be my Lord and Savior for evermore. In Your holy name, Amen."

Don't walk alone. Find a Christian church family. You may need to visit a few, but when God tells you "this is the one," I know you'll feel it—just like Bill did when he first met the freaks that are now his forever best friends.

All praise and honor to you, Most High!

Amen!

Heidi, Dad, Diane, Mom and Billy as a Christian home.

Diane's 8th Grade Confirmation by Pastor Al in the Lutheran Church.

Henry J Pepper Bird in his first pond at the Koehl farm.

Diane playing saxophone at GVSU Band Camp. She is the second sax player from the right in the front row.

My precious and perfect friend Deb with my parents.

Mom helping me get ready to be married for the first time.

Officially married time number one.

My Father—The Wacky Deer Hunter

Grandma June begins the lesson of how to be a rock mason.

Grandma's lessons pay off and the rocks become a wall.

Diane doing Bible Study by day and then her night job—
actually just on Halloween and not for compensation!

Brother Bill and Diane at Wedding Number Two

Wedding Number Three. The Barton Family that God brought together.

Abbie and her new Daddy Bill.

Bill and Diane being married by dad at the bottom
of Bond Falls in Michigan's Upper Peninsula.

Diane and Bill licensed to dive and loving God's creation under the sea.

Diane as the terrible queen at VBS getting a pie in the face.

Wheezie Sludgebucket (center) with Gary and Makenzy having crazy fun.

Just plain wacky Wheezie soon to be up to something silly.

I love my siblings! Heidi, Bill, and Diane

Diane and Bill at Betsy's wedding.

Abbie and Diane at Betsy's wedding.

Dad and mom after marrying Betsy and Dustin.

Abbie and Bill at Parent's Weekend at Abilene Christian University.

Dad wanting mom's ice cream. The nut doesn't fall too far
from the tree. This is where I come from—oh my!

Jessi the famous woman welder!

Betsy's Family: Logan, Dustin, Betsy and Jayse

Becky Barton Rodeo Girl

Abbie's Baby Dolls: Auggie and Kennedy

ABOUT THE AUTHOR

Diane Barton is married to Bill Barton, husband #3, her dream man (98 percent of the time), who was given to her by God. They live in the woods in southwest Michigan where they enjoy watching the amazing wildlife God has created.

She received awards for Outstanding Volunteer Fundraiser, Hospice Volunteer of the Year, and Spirit of Women Award for an Innovative and Inspiring Spirit.

Diane graduated magna cum laude from Western Michigan University with a degree in management where she received the Jeff Robideau Award for outstanding scholastics in business.

She is a Lean Sigma Green Belt and loves continuous improvement and leading team building activities. She has a passion for coaching leaders and employees.

She is the president of the Board of Wings of Hope Hospice. She was the chair of the capital campaign for the Wings Home, a four-bedroom charitable home providing end-of-life care where she currently serves on their board of directors and volunteers providing hands-on patient care to dying individuals in their last six weeks of life.

She has been a church treasurer, Sunday school teacher, teen youth group leader, and church secretary.

She is a child advocate and sponsor for Compassion International and enjoys sharing her experiences on Compassion Sunday or any other day people will listen.

She enjoys serving others and cheering for people and has no limit to her expressions of enthusiasm, storytelling, and fundraising for charitable organizations.

Her passion is speaking to women about forgiveness and sharing her stories of Christ's genuine love and provision in a humorous and passionate way.

She is a forgiven and loved child of God!

https://www.linkedin.com/in/diane-barton-51500511/